The
Four Laws
of
Debt Free
Prosperity

Just five words spell prosperity, success and happiness
-- five words only -- and they are these:
"Spend less than you get."
--Anonymous

When prosperity comes, do not use all of it.
--Confucius

The
Four Laws
of
Debt Free
Prosperity

Blaine Harris
and Charles Coonradt
with Lee Nelson

Chequemate International

Chequemate International®
57 West 200 South #350
Salt Lake City, Utah 84101
800-CHK-MATE

ISBN 0-9652874-0-8

Library of Congress Catalog Number 96-85208

Printed in the United States of America
Fourth Printing, April 1997.

Introduction

When Paul Smith can't pay his bills, including minimum payments on five credit cards, a home equity loan, a first mortgage and a car lease, he takes a midnight stroll seeking answers to his financial woes.

Fate and a strange set of events brings him in contact with Mary Sessions, a retired IRS auditor with a $20 million bank account who takes Paul into her home, dangles a $2 million carrot in front of his nose and begins teaching him the four laws that made her debt free and financially secure.

Based on a true story, Paul discovers that how much a person earns isn't nearly as important in achieving financial security as most people think -- that nearly anyone on any income can achieve debt-free prosperity by applying the four laws in the story.

Taking place over a period of months, the reader accompanies Paul as Mary guides him, one step at a time, down the path leading to debt-free prosperity. By the time the surprise ending unfolds, the reader along with Paul, has mastered the laws which can guide anyone down the same path.

Through an entertaining and captivating story, this book presents the four time-tested laws developed by Blaine Harris for Chequemate International in its financial management programs for individuals, families and home businesses -- launching an economic crusade to change the financial course of America, one family at a time.

The Next Move is Yours!

About the Authors...

Blaine Harris is the founder, CEO and Chairman of the Board of Chequemate International. In addition, he serves as CEO and Chairman of the Board of Automated Compliance & Training, a public corporation, providing safety and health training solutions to major corporations, hospitals, governmental agencies and hotels. Mr. Harris also sits on the Board of Directors of various corporations.

He has been happily married for 34 years to his lovely companion and high school sweetheart. They have three sons and one daughter, all actively involved in the Chequemate System.

Mr. Harris is an alumnus of Idaho State University where he majored in Business and Marketing. Mr. Harris has extensive experience in real estate with his primary focus being commercial and residential project development. From 1986-1991, Mr. Harris served as CEO, Chairman of the Board of Directors and part owner of Help-U-Sell, Inc. In 1991, Mr. Harris formulated and began development of Chequemate International, Inc.

Charles Coonradt, Chairman and CEO of The Game of Work, Inc. is internationally recognized in the fields of productivity and profitability improvement as an author, consultant and speaker.

Chuck's books *The Game of Work* and *Managing the Obvious* have been labeled the most original and useful tools for business to come along since In Search of Excellence. He is a contributing author to the Chicken Soup for the Soul series.

His clients include Pepsi Cola, Fleming Companies, Marker Bindings, Hoechst Celanese, Ralston-Purina, Browning Ferris Industries, and many other Fortune 500 firms. Over one millions managers and supervisors have heard Chuck's unique message. He lives with his wife and children in Park City, Utah.

Dedication

*to those who will commit to become
independent and debt free*

Successful men and women become
successful only because they acquire the habit
of thinking in terms of success.

Definiteness of purpose can, and it should,
so completely occupy the mind that one has no time or space
in the mind for thoughts of failure.
--Napoleon Hill

Acknowledgments

I would like to acknowledge several people who have had a profound impact upon my life. I would not have understood the fundamental concepts of this book with a deep enough passion to make this project and Chequemate® an international reality without help from the following:

First to my parents, who are no longer here, for teaching me that personal integrity is inseparably connected to accountability and responsibility.

To my wife, Elaine, for her unquestioning faith and support for this work and everything else I am involved in.

To my children, for testing, implementing and further documenting the principles taught in this book.

To my daughter, Marci, for her undying loyalty and ongoing technical assistance as developer and coordinator of the data processing facility. To her husband, Ken, who serves as the executive vice president of our company, who left a successful real estate business in northern California four years ago to help us through every step of the development process.

To my son, Chad, who likewise left a successful securities business in Singapore to join us in the summer of 1995.

To our staff, who have spent countless hours to support and develop the refinements reflected in this book.

To our international friends and clients who have patiently and enthusiastically proven the flexibility and durability of these principles.

To Mr. Chuck Coonradt who developed the *Game of Work* and who contributed much to the preparation of this book.

To Lee Nelson, whose writing skill and belief in the *Chequemate®* process enabled us to present the concepts and principles in this book in an easy-to-read and enjoyable format.
Blaine Harris

I want to thank my partner -- that is my life partner, business partner, parenting partner and eternal partner -- my wife, Carla, without whom my life would not have turned out the way it has.

Also thanks to my children, Christina, Kelly, Christopher, Cody and Christian -- without you none of this would have been possible or very important.

Thank you to the thousands of chief executive officers and owners that have retained and used our concepts. These people hired us to teach and, in fact, wound up teaching me.

Thanks to Blaine Harris, for his vision and commitment to the timeless principles of *Chequemate®* -- and for his invitation to be a part of this great work.
Charles Coonradt

Contents

Whatever you can do or dream you can, begin it.
Boldness has genius and magic in it.
Begin it now.
--Goethe

Do not let what you cannot do interfere with what you can do
--John Wooden,
former UCLA basketball coach

Money is plentiful for those who understand the
simple laws which govern its acquisition.
--George Clason

A *Lady Named Mary*

The Paul Smith Story

It was almost 2 a.m. when I went looking for the shotgun. I wasn't a drinker, but I was obsessed with blowing away my sorrows, though I was not the kind of person who would really do something like that. Still, it seemed like the worst night of my life. I could not sit at the desk another minute.

I wasn't in the midst of a life and death struggle with cancer, nor was I embroiled in a nasty divorce. My circumstances were more mundane, but to me every bit as painful as any life and death struggle.

It was the time of the month when I had to spend an evening at my desk paying bills. The evening had started out on a painful note when I examined a yellow card from the post office informing me I had a registered letter from the IRS. I didn't cheat on my taxes, but was worried I had been a little too creative. I was a sales rep for a furniture manufacturer and

1

always seemed to be spending personal money on business without getting receipts. At tax time, I usually gave myself a generous deduction to cover these undocumented expenses. Now I was sure they were going to audit me, and if they told me I had to come up with another $2,000 or go to jail, I wouldn't be able to find $2,000. Pushing the yellow card to the back of the desk, hoping it might get lost, I prayed the custodian at the IRS would inadvertently push my file into a waste basket.

Then, I started the gruesome task of paying bills, beginning with the small ones.

I made minimum payments on the five charge cards, trying to ignore the $10 late fees, and the small print describing finance charges of 18% to 25% on the unpaid balances.

I made an interest-only payment on the home equity loan, then examined a rejection letter from the company where I had applied for a second home equity loan. I had responded to their advertising which claimed, "If you need money, get it out of your house. We give 100%, not 80% like those other home equity companies!" In the rejection letter, they said they couldn't make the loan because I didn't have sufficient income to make the payments. I threw the letter in the trash wondering about the banker mentality - the more you needed money the less they were inclined to loan it to you. It didn't seem fair that money is always more available to those who don't seem to need it.

Then I opened the letter from the vehicle leasing company announcing the lease on my car was finished. I was supposed to turn it in to the leasing dealer along with a check for $1,867 to cover the high mileage penalty. This made me mad. My lease payments were higher than monthly purchase payments would have been, and now I owed almost $2,000 extra. How would I ever find enough money for a down payment on a new car? I was trapped.

In the pile of bills, I found a glimmer of hope. Through a cellophane window on the front of one of the envelopes, I could see my name and address printed on a check. I ripped it open. It

A Lady Named Mary

was a check for $1,500. Who would be sending me that kind of money?

A car dealer. The letter said I could use the check as part of the down payment on a new vehicle. Of course, in order to validate it, I had to show it to the sales manager before I started dealing on the new car. I knew their game. Raise the price $1,500, then send out $1,500 checks to all the suckers like me. I threw the check in the trash.

I paid all the utility bills, but I didn't have enough to make the house payment. I had initiated an overdraw feature on my checking account six months earlier, so the bank would automatically cover overdrafts, but I was already over the $2,000 limit, was paying 18% on the balance, and would have to start making payments on that next month. I had used the last of the overdraw credit to make the house payment the month before, so I couldn't use the overdraft to make the current house payment.

I got up from the desk and tiptoed into the bedroom where my wife, Judy was sleeping. Without turning on the light, I fished around in her purse until I found her checkbook, then returned to my desk, hoping she might have enough balance to cover the house payment.

I wasn't surprised to find no balance at all. Like me, she just wrote checks, hoping she didn't overdraw the account. I had no way of knowing how much she had. She sold real estate, and the spring months had been slow. It had been more than 30 days since her last commission, so I guessed her account was empty, too.

Tucked behind the last check was a piece of white paper, folded up tight. My motivation wasn't so much curiosity as the need to do something, anything, in an effort to control my growing nightmare.

The paper was a receipt from one of those expensive boutique shops where rich women like to browse. The purchased item listed on the receipt was an artificial Christmas tree.

How well I remembered that tree, and the trauma it had

brought into my life at Christmas time. At first, Judy had brought home a live tree. After two nights of unsuccessful attempts to get me to string the lights on it, she expressed her frustration by going to the boutique store and charging $200 on her VISA card to buy that artificial tree with the lights already in place. I was furious, but the tree stayed.

Now as I looked at the receipt, I realized Judy had deceived me. Yes, she had charged $200 on the VISA. She had also given the store a check for $200 and another $200 in cash. She had paid $600 for the tree! And she had disguised the price by splitting up the payment. She normally didn't do things like this. Apparently, putting lights on the tree had been a lot more important to her than I had supposed. I had been insensitive to her needs, and deserved the punishment she had dished out, a $600 Christmas tree. It seemed I hadn't done anything right lately.

When I couldn't find the shotgun, I headed into the garage to get the double-edged lumber axe. It was in the corner with the garden tools. Without putting on the safety goggles, I turned on the grinder and sharpened both edges. Boy, was Judy going to be sorry.

The artificial tree was in one of the plywood cabinets in the garage. I dragged it onto the front lawn and chopped it into little pieces. When there was nothing bigger than six inches, I buried the axe into the little sycamore tree we had been nursing along. Then I decided to take a walk before I did something really dangerous.

My head was a little calmer now. Swinging the big axe had helped, but none of my financial problems had gone away. I needed to find some money, or my life would be in shambles.

I remembered thinking when I had graduated from college, I would have a great life if I worked hard and increased my earnings to about $40,000 a year. That was my dream, and I had achieved it. With commissions and bonuses, my income ranged between $38,000 to $43,000 a year, yet I couldn't afford to buy a wreath for my own funeral. I was wasting a $600 Christmas tree in the middle of the night because I couldn't pay my bills and was more miserable than I had been in my entire life. What was wrong? Where could I find the money to get out of this terrible predicament?

It occurred to me to go back to the house, jerk the axe out of the tree, pull on a ski mask, and see how much money I could extort from the local Seven-Eleven store. Dumb idea!

It was long past midnight, and only one other house in the neighborhood had lights on.

As I walked up Maple Street, I could see an elderly woman through one of the front windows. She was sitting in an overstuffed chair, reading something. The name on the mailbox was M. Sessions. Her first name was Mary. I didn't know her well, only that she had a full time gardener. She drove a late-model Mercedes, and sometimes chauffeurs picked her up. She lived alone in a house that would appraise for more than half a million dollars. I guessed she was in her late sixties or early seventies. In my occasional conversations with her, she had seemed friendly and articulate.

The thought occurred to me that maybe Mrs. Sessions would loan me some money. I wished I had shoveled snow off her walk or invited her over for dinner, but there was no time to butter her up. I needed money now. Mustering courage, I tiptoed onto the porch and knocked on the door.

"Nice to know I'm not the only one who can't sleep," she said brightly, recognizing me as she opened the door.

There was an elegant quality about Mary Sessions. Even though her neatly-cropped hair was gray, there was a vibrant, healthy look about her. Her eyes were the color of Navajo turquoise, and had an intense, piercing quality, rarely found in 19-year-olds. She had fewer wrinkles than women half her age, even in the middle of the night with no make-up.

I asked her if she had any 12-gauge shotgun shells.

"What in the world for?" she asked, laughing. I was

5

pleased that she found my comment funny.

Quickly, in my mind, I condensed my financial predicament and blurted it out, ending with, "If I don't find some money fast, I'll need shotgun shells to blow my brains out."

There was a lighthearted tone in my voice as I made this last statement. I didn't want her to think I was really serious, but deep down in my heart, I think if she had handed me shotgun shells, I would have been sorely tempted to use them.

"You are asking me for a loan?" she asked.

"Yes, I think money would be better than blowing my brains out."

"I have never loaned money to a neighbor before," she said, hesitating. "But I suppose there's a first time for everything. Would you like to come in?" Pushing the door all the way open, she stepped back, allowing me to enter.

"Mr. Smith, how much do you need?" she asked. "Please call me Paul. I think ten thousand would stop the bleeding," I said, suddenly wishing I hadn't said it, feeling ashamed at my audacity for dropping such a request at three in the morning on a 70-year-old woman I hardly knew.

She began to laugh.

"What's wrong?" I asked.

"Nothing," she said. "I'm just relieved. A neighbor shows up in the middle of the night asking for shotgun shells or money, so I naturally assume he needs some real money, not just pocket change. Glad I was wrong."

Who was this woman who thought ten thousand dollars was pocket change?

"Twenty thousand would stop the bleeding and put a nice dressing on the wound," I said, suddenly feeling greedy enough to double my request.

"First you ask for ten, then for twenty. Sounds like you really don't know how much you need," she said. "No wonder the bank wouldn't give you money."

I had the sick feeling I had just blown a wonderful

opportunity. I should not have been greedy.

"How did you know the bank wouldn't give me money?" I asked, suspecting that perhaps she owned the bank.

"Just a hunch," she winked. "Would you like to play some chess while we work this out?"

My idea of fun did not include playing chess in the middle of the night with a woman old enough to be my mother. But if a little chess would get me a loan, why not?

"Sure," I said, with pretended enthusiasm.

We seated ourselves on sofas at opposite ends of a coffee table. The playing board and pieces were already in place. I decided to let her win, thinking that might improve my chances of getting the money.

We hadn't been playing very long when she went over to a desk, shuffled through one of the drawers, then returned with a little book in her hand. It was a passbook for a savings account.

"Most of my money is in stocks, bonds and real estate," she explained, "but I keep a little bit in a savings account for emergencies." She tossed the passbook on the table in front of me, nodding for me to look inside. I did so, carefully memorizing the balance. $147,952.34.

"I suppose your coming here could be considered an emergency," she offered.

"It is for me," I said, very sincerely, still holding onto the passbook, hardly daring to hope that Mary Sessions might actually give me money.

As we continued the game of chess, I realized I didn't have to let her win. She was going to win whether I wanted to let her or not.

"Look," she said thoughtfully, when we were almost finished, "I don't like throwing good money after bad."

My hopes sank into the bottom of my shoes. She wasn't going to give me the money, after all.

"I would feel a lot better about loaning you money if I thought it would do some good," she countered.

"Oh, it will," I assured her. "I'll make my house payment, buy hamburger and potatoes for the children to eat. None of it will be spent frivolously."

"You probably think I'm a silly old widow with more money than sense," she said.

"Oh no," I lied, wondering how she could read my mind.

"We were a month behind on the rent when my husband died," she said, suddenly changing the direction of our conversation. She leaned back, forgetting the chess game.

"I'm sorry."

"I don't need your sympathy, not anymore. I had three small children, no insurance, no savings, and no marketable skills. Do you have any idea what it is like getting food for your children in the trash bins behind grocery stores? When the clerks caught me, I told them I was looking for produce for my pet pig."

I couldn't believe what I was hearing. I tried hard to picture this elegant woman foraging through trash bins in search of food scraps for her babies. I couldn't imagine.

"But, what about all this?" I asked, pointing to the expensive surroundings, and the passbook. "How did you get from there to here? And don't tell me you worked really hard. I know a lot of people who work hard and never accomplish anything like this. I'm one of them."

"I didn't start out with a $40,000-a-year job like you have," she said. "You have no idea how blessed you are. There are a lot of people who would do anything for the chance to get $40,000 a year driving around in a new car, calling on furniture stores."

"If my job is so wonderful, why am I so miserable and so broke?"

"It's one thing to work hard, and quite another to work smart. Do you really want to know how I did it, and how you can do it too?"

"Of course."

"Do you think you can trust an old woman?"

"What does that have to do with anything?" I asked.

"If I am going to help you, teach you, and loan you money, I have to know everything about your financial life. You will have to trust me, like you would a banker asking for financial information. Do you think you can do that?"

"You want financial statements, balance sheets, stuff like that?" I asked.

"And more."

"Like what?" I asked. She got up and went over to the desk. She returned with another savings passbook, but when she handed it to me, I could see this one was blank.

"Write your name on it," she said.

"Am I going to open a savings account?" I asked, hoping she had decided to make a deposit in my name.

"No," she said. "We can't determine how much you need until we know how much you have and how you are spending it. For the next 30 days, I want you to track your daily expenses and every other financial transaction by writing them down. If you spend 50 cents for a Coke, write it down in this book. If you charge gas on your VISA, write it down. If you write a check, make a deposit or a withdrawal from the money machine, write it down. I want every financial transaction in your life written down in this little book."

"You're asking a lot," I complained.

"Two or three minutes a day, at most," she shot back. "If you are not willing to do that, then leave right now and never come back."

"I'll do it," I promised.

"Checkmate," she said, yawning while making her last move. It was getting light outside. It was time for me to leave.

"What about my house? I can't make the payment. You said you would loan me money. What about that?" I realized I was being pushy, but I was desperate.

"You won't lose your house in 30 days," she said. "It will

take at least that long for you to master the discipline of tracking daily expenses."

"Then you will loan me the money?" I was determined to pin her down, get an answer, one way or the other.

"As I said earlier," she responded, thoughtfully, "I don't like throwing good money away. Until you learn the laws of financial success, you frankly are a bad credit risk."

"I suppose there are fifty laws," I said, starting to feel that I had gotten my hopes up for nothing. The old woman was toying with me.

"Altogether, I suppose there could be that many, perhaps more. But there are only four main laws," she said, beginning to rub her chin, thoughtfully. There was a long silence as we looked into each other's eyes. I had no idea what was going on in her head, only that something serious was happening, and it would be best for me not to disturb the silence.

"I'll tell you what I'll do," she said, finally, her words slow and deliberate. "When you have demonstrated to me that you have mastered the four laws, I'll loan you all the money you want."

"I don't believe you," I said, emotion in my voice. I felt like I was going to cry. She had no right to toy with me like this.

"You don't trust me?" she asked.

"Get real," I said, starting to feel angry. "Remember the days when you were scrounging in the garbage bins? If a grocery clerk had offered to give you all the money you wanted, would you have believed him? Or would you have laughed at him?"

"I would have slapped him for being so cruel," she said.

"Now you know how I feel." Again there was a long pause as we looked into each other's eyes.

"I'll put it in writing," she said, turning and walking over to the desk. All I wanted to do was go home, but I waited in silence as she scribbled something on a piece of paper.

When she finally handed me the paper, I could hardly believe what I was reading.

A Lady Named Mary

To Whom it May Concern:

Being of sound mind, I, Mary Sessions, do hereby agree to loan money to my neighbor, Paul Smith, when he has demonstrated to my satisfaction that he has mastered the four laws of financial success. No collateral will be required for said loan. The interest rate will be 8%; the terms of payback will be negotiated at the time the loan is made, and the amount shall not exceed $2,000,000.

Mary Sessions, February 29, 1995

I was speechless. Carefully I folded up the paper and placed it in my pocket, along with the blank passbook. As I walked home, I had the strongest feeling that Mary Sessions was going to change my life. I was determined to do all she asked. I also decided I needed to impress her by winning the next chess game.

*The financial record-keeping functions essential to the success
and survival of any business are equally beneficial and
necessary in the financial lives of individuals
and families.*
--Blaine Harris

School Begins

After a few days of recording every financial transaction, I dropped in on Mary one evening to show her my passbook and what I was doing. She was right. It took only a few minutes a day, but I didn't like doing something that sometimes seemed so trivial and tedious. She seemed pleased that I came to see her, and wanted to play another game of chess, but I said I didn't have time.

"But isn't it a little silly recording every donut, Coke and quarter for the parking meter?" I asked, attempting to express my frustration.

She invited me to sit down beside her on one of the sofas. Thoughtfully, she rubbed some of the aging spots on her left hand.

"Tracking daily expenses is the first necessary step toward any kind of financial success," she said. "A good business records every financial transaction in basically the same way you

13

are doing it. Every penny coming in and every penny going out is accounted for, in writing. From this raw data, the many reports for management, stockholders and tax collectors are assembled.

"I had a friend who was an accountant for Ford Motor Company. He said the company kept three sets of books; one for management, one for stock holders, and one for the IRS. *Without the raw data from every financial transaction, and the resulting reports and documents, no business can survive.*

"You have to be able to count it or measure it if you want to manage it. *How can you tell if you are winning or losing if you don't keep score?* Doesn't it make sense that the financial principles that are absolutely essential for the success and survival of any business are of equal value in managing the finances of private individuals and families?"

"Yes," I said, and started to get up. She motioned for me to stay put.

"You see, businesses and wealthy people hire accountants and bookkeepers to track their money. Poor people don't. That's one of the reasons they stay poor. You think you are not wealthy enough to hire an accountant, so I am teaching you how to do it yourself.

"You see," she continued, "That which we focus on daily becomes easy or automatic. It's not that the nature of the task becomes easier, but your ability to handle it increases. A basketball player who will spend a few hours every day practicing shooting and fundamentals in a tough game situation, will find himself on automatic pilot so he doesn't have to think about what he is doing. He doesn't have time to think. Finances are the same way. If you spend a little time every day doing fundamental stuff, like recording expenditures, you'll find yourself on automatic pilot, and in control, when the tough problems come along. Your ability to handle big financial problems increases as you expend daily effort on fundamentals."

As she talked, I had the feeling that she was telling me things I already knew, things buried in some deep forgotten place. Her words were bringing truth to the surface.

"Over the years I've learned to keep my weight down," she continued. "It wasn't easy, but one of the strange phenomena of dieting is if you can discipline yourself to write down on a piece of paper the calorie count in every item of food you eat, and if you don't do anything else, you begin to lose weight. The process of counting calories alone will bring about a weight loss. Isn't that interesting?"

"Are you trying to tell me that merely writing down my financial transactions will ease my financial problems?"

"Absolutely. You will find money that's been slipping through the cracks. Tracking helps you see the cracks, so you can plug them up, so you can have more money for the important things."

"Good," I said, getting up to leave. "I'll keep tracking."

Again, she motioned for me to sit back down. "There's more."

"The best computer in the world is the one between your ears," she began. "Everyone has a personal computer more powerful than anything at the Pentagon, but most people don't give their internal computers a fair chance to help them, especially when it comes to finances." She reached forward, picked up one of the castles on the chess board and began playing with it.

"The computer in your head can't help with your finances if you don't give it the raw data to work with. And you can't second guess your computer by giving it limited information. It doesn't play its best game with a partial deck. It has capabilities far beyond your conscious abilities. Don't limit its effectiveness by giving it partial or limited data. Give it everything. Give it the data from every financial transaction in your life, then stand back and let it go to work for you. You will be amazed at how much better you will be at solving your financial problems. Go home and track everything. Get your wife and children to do it too."

"Fat chance of that ever happening," I said. "They are a lot worse at managing money than I am."

"Next time you and Judy discuss the household and grocery budget, give her one of these little passbooks, and ask her to record her transactions. Tell her in a month you will add up the transactions and go over them with her, and together you can decide if anything needs to be changed.

Do the same thing with the children and their $20 allowances, but tell them if they can only account for half of what you give them, when allowance time rolls around again, you will give them only half as much. Their monthly allowances will equal the total of the transactions in their books, not to exceed the $20 received at the beginning of the month. Be tough, but not mean. They'll come around."

As I walked home that evening I was determined to become a tracking fanatic. I wrote down everything for a month. Judy and the children, with the expected protest, wrote down most things. I didn't show them the $2,000,000 promissory note. That was my private secret, my private hope.

I began to make some interesting discoveries, like Judy and I running up between $85 and $100 a month in overdrawn check charges. That was as stupid as using $20 bills to test paper shredders. We put a stop to it.

I also discovered Judy and the children were renting two or three videos three or four nights a week, costing us nearly $100 a month. Many of the videos we didn't even watch. Using the argument that the children needed to be doing better in school, I set the rule that videos could be checked out only on Friday or Saturday night, unless special circumstances approved by me and Judy dictated otherwise. This saved another $75. By the end of the month I had an extra $300 and was able to pay all the bills, but I was still a month behind on the house payment.

If you can't measure it, you can't manage it.
--George Odiorne

The First Law

Not only did I become addicted to tracking, recording in the little passbook every penny that passed in and out of my possession, but I insisted that Judy and the children keep doing it, too. Since a good portion of my income passed through their hands, it was essential for them to be involved. Of course, they were not as excited about the process as I was, and they couldn't understand why I was suddenly so determined to track every penny in our household. They still didn't know about the $2,000,000 carrot Mary Sessions was dangling in front of my nose. I didn't want to use that to bring them around. I would tell them later. It would be a wonderful surprise.

The idea that fascinated me was Mary's claim that the process of tracking, by itself, would improve our financial situation -- like counting calories helped keep her weight down.

One night while browsing through my library I found a neat tracking story in a book titled, *The Game of Work,* by Chuck

Chequemate

Coonradt, in which Lee Nelson related how this tracking helped him in a teenage work experience. Following is the story in Lee's own words.

My first real contact with (tracking)...occurred one afternoon during my first after-school job as a bag boy at a Safeway grocery store in Walnut Creek, California, earning $1.33 an hour. It was probably the first or second day of my employment when the assistant manager took me into the back room and showed me three 4X8 plywood bins filled to overflowing with empty pop bottles.

The assistant manager explained that the bottles needed to be sorted by kind into cases before they could be picked up by the various vendors. He explained why there were so many bottles in the bins, that the adult clerks hated to "work bottles," and avoided the task whenever possible. That was why I was being given the job -- as a 16-year-old kid, I was at the bottom of the pecking order.

The manager introduced me to the corner of the back room designated for sorting bottles. He showed me where the empty cases were stored, which bottles could be combined in the same cases, and which had to be kept separate, and where the cases of empties needed to be stacked. Just when I thought I knew all there was to know about the new task, and was ready to go to work, the manager said, "It takes most clerks one hour to do a bin. I hope you can do that well."

He looked at his watch. I looked at mine.

"Let me know when you finish the first bin," he said, then added, "Some of the bottles have left-over pop, help yourself." He smiled at his sick attempt at humor, then turned and walked away.

Suddenly, my work had meaning. Working the bottles was not just another job that needed to be done. A standard had been set by which my performance would be measured. My progress was being tracked. The manager was keeping score on my efforts. I was keeping score too. My palms began to sweat. I looked at the bins of bottles with new interest.

Tracking

Comparing working bottles with my favorite sport, basketball, the manager had put me into a real game situation and turned on the scoreboard. In corporate terminology, he had ordered the accountants to track and report the progress in my department. I flew at the bottles.

An hour and ten minutes later I finished the first bin, frustrated at my clumsiness, but confident that if I persisted I could beat the magic 60-minute barrier -- the accepted standard in my new working world.

I became the designated bottle worker in that store, delighting the clerks who hated this work. A record was kept on how long it took me to work each bin of bottles. After about a month, I worked three overflowing bins of bottles in one hour -- three times the acceptable rate set by the clerks. The manager was pleased. The other workers talked about it.

I believed I was possibly the fastest bottle worker in the entire Safeway chain. I felt like I had accomplished something significant. Maybe the other workers knew more than me about checking, cutting meat or trimming lettuce -- but I knew more about working bottles, and could do my job at least twice as fast as anyone else in the store. Because my performance had been measured and reported back, it had improved beyond anyone's expectations.

The manager of the night stocking crew heard about the kid with the fast hands and arranged for me to be promoted to the position of night stock clerk as soon as school was out. The night crew worked from 11 p.m. until 8 a.m., and my hourly wage was increased to $2.42 per hour.

The night manager had a competitive personality, on and off the job. Every task was a race to see who was best and fastest. At the end of a night's work, a typical comment was, "Big load coming in today. Better wear your runnin' shoes tonight."

When I arrived to begin work, he would say how many cases arrived on the truck that afternoon. "Only 721 cases today. Ought to be through about 4:30." Then we'd go to work.

Chequemate

My eyes couldn't keep up with his price marker as it flew over the cans. He could throw six soup cans at a time onto the shelf, three in each hand, the labels all facing forward when the cans came to rest in perfect rows. As much as he loved speed, he never sacrificed quality. On Tuesday night when we washed and waxed the floors, his mop could perform more tricks than a witch's broom. He had learned that in the Navy.

The night manager challenged me to try to keep up with him, an impossible task at first. But I tried very hard, and every week got a little closer. It seemed every task was timed and measured, even the tearing up of boxes for the incinerator. Speed and accuracy were the game, and we kept score. It made the work fun, like sports. I liked to go to work.

Some of the night crew workers didn't like to compete with the manager and me. They thought we were too "gung ho." They seemed to prefer watching the clock instead of beating it.

It felt good to walk outside after a night's work, my body winding down after running to keep up with or beat the manager, then hear him throw down the challenge to come back that night with my running shoes. His words were music to my ears. I felt like an athlete getting ready for the big game.

Sometimes I think back on that first experience with the bottles, and wonder how things might have turned out if the manager had merely told me to go in the back room and work bottles until quitting time, and had not tracked my progress.

Lee's story supports the universal truth that *when performance is measured, performance improves because the performers try harder and have more fun.* George Odiorne said, "If you can't measure it, you can't manage it."

One Wednesday night, Judy announced that because of some volunteer work she had been involved in, she had received four tickets to a figure skating competition in the city on the upcoming Saturday night.

"What a strange coincidence," I said, explaining that at work that afternoon my company had given four ice hockey tickets to each sales rep who reached his quota the previous

Tracking

month. The hockey game was Saturday night too, and it was just a few blocks from the figure skating competition.

My son Billy and I wanted to go to the hockey game. But Judy and our daughter Lisa wanted to go to the figure skating competition.

"I can't understand why anyone would rather watch a bunch of guys fighting on the ice over the beauty and grace of figure skating," Judy argued.

"Hockey players are better athletes," Billy protested. "They skate circles around those guys in tights."

"They cannot," Lisa shot back. And so the discussion began, lasting an hour or more. I'm not sure who won. It just seemed refreshing to see the family doing something like this instead of watching television. The end result was that we decided to go to both events -- the first part of the figure skating, and the second half of the hockey game.

I enjoyed the figure skating more than I thought I would. Even Billy offered polite applause with everyone else when each skater, or pair of skaters, finished, and when the judges held up the cards with the individual scores ranging from about 4.5 to 6.5. The skaters politely accepted the judges' evaluations, whether they were happy about the scores or not.

At one point a pretty 16-year-old girl fell down during the last part of her routine. She started to cry. There were oohs and ahs in the audience as people felt sorry for the poor girl. After her performance, when one of the judges, a bald man in a white turtle neck sweater, held up a score card with 4.5 written on it, Billy was the only one who booed.

The hockey game was different. The first time a player fell hard on the ice, the crowd hardly noticed, except for Billy who made a few oohs and ahs, imitating the figure skating crowd. Then he brought our attention to the fact that the player on the ice had not begun to cry.

"Oh shut up," Lisa said.

Billy noticed other differences, like when an official made

21

a particularly questionable call, the players complained and the fans booed. Some threw cups of beer at the official.

"Wish I'd had a cup of beer to throw at that bald-headed idiot in the white turtleneck," Billy said.

Later, one of the players was put in the penalty box for tripping up the beer-soaked official. There were two or three good fights during the match, and whenever the home team scored, the fans went wild. The players skated hard, and the fans were loud during the final period, with the home team behind by a single goal.

On the way home we had a lively discussion over the differences in the two ice skating competitions we had witnessed. Both events involved skilled athletes who had spent many years preparing to perform.

I suggested that perhaps the reason the figure skating crowd and performers were so polite was the fact that nobody knew the score until the performance was over, and it was too late to do anything about it. I pointed out that the reason the final period of the hockey match was so wild was because the home team was one goal behind. The players were skating harder to catch up, and the fans were cheering them on. I speculated that if a figure skater knew she was half a point down while she was performing, she would skate harder in an effort to catch up.

The fans at a figure skating event don't know what is happening either. They don't know if a particular skater is falling behind, catching up, or not even in the running -- so the applause is polite. When the judges finally hold up their score cards, the performance is over, and it is too late to do anything.

"With computer technology the way it is," Billy suggested, "they ought to develop a system where each judge has an electronic scoreboard above his head, and a dial with 1-10 numbering, so whichever number the judge turns to, that is the number on the score board. All the boards read five when the performance begins, and the judges would turn their dials up or down as the performance develops. The fans and skaters would then know the score during the performance and could react accordingly. The fans, being able to see the changing numbers, would know whether or not to cheer or boo. The skater could become more aggressive in an effort to catch up, or more conservative in an effort to protect a comfortable lead.

Lisa pointed out that the girl cried when she fell down, not because she was a girl and the fall hurt, but because she knew the judges were lowering her score. "Hockey players would cry, too," she added, "if the officials took a point off the scoreboard every time one of them fell down."

"They would not," Billy argued.

Suddenly, I saw an opportunity to tie all of this in with our family finances. "The big difference between figure skating and ice hockey is the score keeping," I said. "In figure skating nobody knows the score until the performance is over, so the crowd is polite, and the performer is careful. When the judges finally hold up their cards, the results are so subjective, the high and low scores are thrown out. It's a bad system, but I guess it's all we have until someone like Billy comes up with something better."

"On the other hand," I continued, "in ice hockey the fans, the players, and the officials know the score at all times. The official can't change the score if a player hits him with a stick, or if a fan throws a cup of beer at him. The play changes as a team aggressively tries to catch up, or becomes more defensive in protecting a lead."

"It's more fun when everybody knows the score," Billy added.

"Exactly," I said. "That's why I have been trying to get all of us to keep score with our family finances. It's no fun to lose. Every month when I sit down to pay the bills, and don't have enough money to pay them all, I realize we've lost again."

I told them what Mary had promised, that if we would keep score on a daily basis by tracking all of our financial transactions, we would start winning the money game. I said I was determined to do that, and needed their help and cooperation.

Lisa asked if we could still afford the vacation to Yellowstone we had been talking about. I said we would still go on the vacation if we could pay for it with cash. I would not charge a vacation on a 20% VISA card. Furthermore, the first 10% of every paycheck was already committed to paying ourselves first, and that money at the present time was committed to getting rid of our debts. If we could find the vacation money in the remaining 90% of my income allocated to living expenses, then we could still do the vacation. Judy suggested we set up a special savings account for vacations. I agreed to do it.

"I reminded them that as we persisted in tracking all of our expenses, we would discover expenses that were not as important as our family vacation. These expenses could be eliminated or reduced, and that's how we would find the money we needed. But everyone had to help."

As a parent you always wonder if serious discussions like these sink in. But in the coming weeks I realized an impact had been made. Billy bought a new pair of basketball shoes at Payless for about half the price we had previously paid for name-brand Air Jordan type shoes. He insisted we put the difference in our vacation account. At prom time, Lisa borrowed a dress instead of buying a new one, on the condition we would put the dress money into the vacation account. As the end of school approached, we realized that even though the vacation might not happen until August, it was indeed going to take place without going further into debt.

Billy and I found ourselves in an ongoing discussion about tracking and score keeping in sports. We noticed the score is almost always the first thing the news reports about any sporting event. Everybody wants to know who won, by how much, and which players scored the most points. Every sport has score cards, scoreboards and stat sheets.

Tracking

In sports, especially professional sports, measurements are continually added to increase player performance and fan interest in the game. Baseball has what they call the slugging percentage, in addition to the batting average and runs batted in. In golf they have driving accuracy measurements, putting percentages, number of greens hit and putts per round. Some basketball coaches are monitoring points per possession in an effort to measure the effectiveness of both offensive and defensive strategies. Good coaches understand that *when performance is measured, performance improves.*

We discussed how these principles apply to money. If you measure and track every dollar, if you keep score, you will play the game better, your win/loss percentage will go up.

One day I tried to explain all this to a co-worker who decided to go home and look over his bank statement. He discovered the health insurance package he had canceled more than a year earlier, was still activating the automatic monthly withdrawal. He thought he had canceled the policy with a phone call when he had started another policy. For over a year he had been paying on both policies, wasting or throwing away over $2,000 in duplicate insurance fees. The first company wouldn't refund the money because they had no written record of a cancellation. *Had he been tracking his expenses on a regular basis, this would not have happened.*

In time I realized good things were happening in my family. The children, especially, were learning to manage money, something they didn't seem to learn in school.

You can ask anyone which is most important, their family, or their job or business, and they will look at you funny as if wondering why you would ask a question where the answer is so obvious. Of course, the family is more important than the job or business.

If the family is more important, then why don't we manage family finances with the same care, detail and professionalism used in managing business finances? *If businesses ran their finances the way most families do, the business failure rate would skyrocket.*

What most of us don't seem to understand is that progress in our financial lives, not just sports and business, is directly related to the ability to measure. Four hundred years ago the most portable mechanical timepiece was a water clock on a wagon. It was 10 feet high, weighed 300 pounds, and you had to pull it around with a horse. And it didn't keep good time if the water slopped around. The smallest unit of length measurement was the distance from King Henry's thumb to his nose, a yard. Everything they built was designed around that unit of measurement. The "rule of thumb" was a law prohibiting men from beating their wives with sticks bigger around than a thumb.

Today we are much better at measuring things. We have memory chips and integrated circuits. Our ability to measure and keep track of numbers is growing faster than anyone ever guessed. In the mid-1980s, Microsoft chief, Bill Gates said, "64K ought to be enough for anyone." By the mid 90s 64K computers were more obsolete than manual typewriters.

Thanks to computers, almost anyone, on a daily basis, can know how much interest they are paying, or earning, and exactly how much money they still owe on debts. It is even possible for private individuals with modest incomes to receive timely printed reports each month giving the exact status of financial goals, a dollar-by-dollar account of spending for the month, and updated balance and income statements. *For the cost of going out to dinner, anyone can have a personal accounting and score keeping system comparable in value to those enjoyed by billionaires and major corporations.*

One of the greatest rituals in America occurs at lunch when three or four friends get together to eat, and enjoy each other's company.

"How are things going?" someone asks.

"Great, except I have a little bit of a cash flow problem. Sure hope one of you picks up the tab today."

Tracking

Everyone nods with solemn understanding. "Boy, we sure know what that's like. Why is it that everybody seems to have a cash flow problem?"

What are these guys talking about? Cash doesn't flow, not like water. Dollars are made of paper, or are numbers on a pay check or bank statement. Cash isn't water, nor does it flow like water.

People who work for minimum wage, or people who don't work at all, are the only ones entitled to complain about cash flow. The rest of us should quit trying to hide in the foggy world of euphemisms because we are too lazy to track our daily expenses.

Instead of saying he has a cash flow problem, the guy should tell his friends he is too lazy or too stupid to do simple arithmetic.

"What do you mean?" they ask.

"I suppose if I had the ability to add up the sum total of my take home pay in two paychecks each month, then I'd know how much I could spend, instead of always going over. And I suppose if I wasn't too lazy to use that check register booklet they send me every time I order new checks, I could see how much money is going out, and pace myself so I'm not always running out before the end of the month. I don't have the backbone and courage to live within my means. I deserve a tuna fish sandwich in my pocket instead of coming to this fine restaurant with my friends. I'm an idiot."

"We understand," the others say, "because we run our finances that way too. But we think you are a little hard on yourself when you say you are an idiot."

"Then what should I call myself?" the first guy asks.

"How about Uncle Sam?" someone chirps in, and they all have a good laugh, but nobody goes home and changes the sloppy way he handles his money.

There is no such thing as a cash flow problem. Adolph Hitler's propaganda minister Joseph Goebbels said that if a lie is repeated long enough and loud enough everybody will believe it. That's the way it is with cash flow. *Smart people look past the euphemism and find the exact places where their cash flew when they thought it was going to flow.* They backtrack along the cash pipeline looking for the leaks, knowing that if they can find the leaks, they can fix them.

You've got to measure it before you can manage it. Like in the bottle story at the beginning of this chapter, when performance is measured, it improves. When it is measured and reported back, the rate of improvement accelerates, a principle explained by Thomas Monson in a book many years ago.

Tracking -- The first law of debt-free prosperity

"Personal goal setting is the strongest force in the world."
--Paul J. Meyer

The Second Law

Proudly, I made my report to Mary. As we began our second game of chess, I told her about the registered letter from the IRS at the post office, and how I was worried about being audited and having my personal business deductions disallowed because I didn't have receipts.

"Next year you won't have to worry about that," she said. "You'll have all your personal transactions recorded in these little books."

"But what do I do now?" I asked.

"Open it. It may not be as bad as you think." She began to laugh.

"What's so funny?" I asked.

"That you are so afraid of the IRS?"

"If you were in my shoes, you would be afraid too."

"No I wouldn't."

"Why?"

"I used to be an IRS auditor."

"Really?" I asked, reaching for the passbook, thinking I

had better be moving along. Suddenly, I felt very uncomfortable knowing I had been spilling out the secrets of my financial troubles to an IRS agent.

"Those nights I was fishing through the dumpsters, I was studying accounting," she explained. "When I got my degree, the IRS gave me a job. I became an auditor."

"People working for the IRS don't make enough money to live like this," I challenged. "They certainly don't make enough to make $2,000,000 unsecured loans to neighbors."

"They do if they use their money wisely," she argued.

"What is that supposed to mean?"

"My job was to review tax returns. I saw the returns of the rich and the poor. I saw teachers earning less than $20,000 a year who were financially independent. I saw doctors earning $200,000 a year who were at the edge of bankruptcy. I was always amazed at how one person earning $40,000 a year could live so much better than another earning the same amount. Studying thousands of returns every year, I learned some valuable lessons.

"While auditing the records of very successful people, I made some good friends and learned some valuable lessons. I saw where smart people put their money and where other people squandered theirs.

"I built a $20 million net worth, not from my IRS paycheck but from what I did with my savings from those paychecks. But that's enough for tonight. Open the registered letter. It may not be as bad as you think."

"Checkmate," she said, winning our second game of chess.

She was right. The letter informed me that I had made an error and owed them an additional $431. Mary told me to send them $75 with a note saying I would send them that amount every month until the debt was paid in full.

After two months of tracking my financial transactions, I went over to Mary's for a third game of chess. I told her I had called the leasing company and proposed I drive my car for another year, if they would lower the payment amount and apply the difference to what I owed them for high mileage. They accepted my offer.

I told her tracking had helped a lot, and I was willing to continue doing it, but I still had too many money problems. I told her I was ready to learn the second law.

She said *the second law was setting targets or goals.*

"We have already talked about the computer between your ears," Mary began. "Through your tracking you are putting a lot of financial information into your computer that it doesn't know how to process yet. It doesn't know what to look for. It doesn't know to what end you want this financial data manipulated.

"You have to give your computer targets or goals. Then it goes to work manipulating the data you input to help you achieve those goals."

"Then I set my goal to have $50 billion in six months," I said.

"Don't mock me," she said as we seated ourselves on opposite sides of the chess board.

"Then my goal is to beat you at chess," I said.

"That's about as likely as finding $50 billion," she challenged as she moved the first pawn.

"They always talk about goal setting at our sales meetings," I explained. "I guess I never paid much attention or believed it to be anything more than a gimmick used by management to get salesmen to work harder for less money. I don't have any financial goals beyond putting out today's fires."

"How much do you pay a month in interest on all your debt?" she asked, after four or five moves.

"About $1,200 a month," I said, without having to think very hard. The tracking had made me much more aware of where my money was going.

"How would you like it if your employer gave you a $1,000 a month after-tax raise?" she asked.

"My financial worries would be gone. Fat chance that

would ever happen," I complained.

"Then give it to yourself. You don't even have to tell your employer."

"I don't understand. Do you want me to steal or embezzle?"

"Of course not. Just get out of debt. Not paying $1,200 a month in interest is just like getting a $1,000 a month after tax raise. Why don't you do that for yourself?"

"I can give you about eight reasons," I said. "There's a house mortgage, a home equity loan, five charge cards, a checking account overdraft note and a debt to a leasing company. My monthly payments barely cover the interest let alone the principal. I'm going to have to go further in debt when I buy a new car. Then the kids will be going to college. I am resigned to being in debt the rest of my life. There's no other way."

"Would you like to be out of debt and have that extra $1,000 a month?" she asked.

"Certainly, who wouldn't want that?"

"Most people don't seem to care. Otherwise they would do something about it."

"Most people probably don't know what to do," I added.

"If I could show you how to get completely out of debt in less than five years, without increasing your income, would you want to select being debt free as one of your targets?"

"More than anything," I said, "but how is that possible when I can barely make my interest payments?"

"In order for you to understand how easy it would be for you to get out of debt, you need to understand the third law. But before we talk about that, we need to finish this discussion about targets or goals. Should we pick being debt free as your first target?"

"Sure," I said. "I guess I'll just have to take your word that it's possible."

She walked over to her desk, picked up a piece of paper and a pen, and brought them back to me.

"Write down your first goal," she said.

"Why?" I asked. "You don't think I could forget something like getting out of debt?"

"A goal that is not written down is just a wish," she explained. I wrote down, on the paper, that I was going to be out of debt in less than five years.

"Every day you see things you want," she explained. "A fancy car, a Caribbean vacation, a bigger home, a beautiful race horse..."

"Wait a minute! I'm not into horses."

"It doesn't matter. No matter what you want, you have to help your internal computer set priorities among all the desires and wants you keep throwing at it," she continued. "You want it to know that getting out of debt is more important than getting a new set of golf clubs. You do this by writing down your high priority targets, then reviewing them frequently, especially before you go to sleep at night and first thing in the morning. If you keep telling your computer that getting out of debt is your first and most important financial target, it will get the message and go to work manipulating all the financial data you are feeding it to help you get out of debt. Do you have any other financial goals?"

"No."

"You said something about your children going to college in a few years. Do you think establishing a fund to help them get a good education would be a good second goal?"

"Sure," I said. "But I don't know how I can do that. I'll just have to trust you." I wrote down something about having a college fund with $30,000 in it by the time my oldest child started college. I had no idea how this could ever happen.

"How about retirement money for you and Judy?" she asked.

"An extra $2,000 a month on top of Social Security would be nice," I said.

"Nice?"

Chequemate

"Wonderful. We wouldn't have to worry about money, or be a burden on the children in our old age."

"Write it down," she said. I did it, then told her I didn't want more than these three goals to worry about. She told me to put the original target or goal sheet in my files after I had made two copies, one for my calendar and appointment book where it would be easy to look at during my travels, and one to put by my bed where I could look at it every night and morning. I agreed to do what she asked, thinking setting targets wouldn't be any harder than tracking daily expenses. But I also knew that *setting* targets, and *achieving* targets were two different things.

"So what's the third law?" I asked. "Or are you going to make me wait?"

"Checkmate," she said, catching me by surprise, and winning our third chess match. Now that we were finished playing, she wanted me to go. She said she would tell me about the third law after I had a chance to study goals and goal achieving techniques for a while. So I went to the library and checked out a dozen books on goals and began my study.

Many people do not have goals, or their goals are too trivial. Few people realize the power in setting a goal, then developing a plan to achieve that goal.

If the lecturer in a financial planning seminar, attended by ordinary working people, asks how many would like to become millionaires, the men in the audience smile, thinking the lecturer is telling a joke. The women frown because they are thinking, "Don't tease me. If you knew anything about becoming a millionaire, you'd be one yourself, relaxing on a beach in southern France, instead of here in Detroit talking to a bunch of idiots who can't pay their phone bills."

In addition to winning the lottery, or finding your name on the will of a rich uncle, the simplest way to become a millionaire is to save $300 a month during your 40-year working career. If you do that you'll have one million in cash the day you retire. If you earn $25,000 a year, the $300 a month is 15% of your income, the same amount saved by the average Japanese worker. Ever wonder why there are so many Japanese tourists at Disneyland and the national parks? Most of them are millionaires when they retire!

You can do it too if you can save $300 a month, about as much as most car payments. It doesn't cost you any more to become a millionaire than to drive a new car. If you can afford a new car, you can afford to become a millionaire.

But everybody doesn't want to be a millionaire. Some of us just want enough so we are not worrying about money all the time. We need enough to pay for our childrens' education, own a comfortable home, be out of debt, be able to retire when we choose to instead of when we have to, and have enough in a retirement fund so, in our old age, we won't be a burden to our children. If you only want these things, you might as well set your sights on being a millionaire because that's how much you will need to accomplish these goals. But you can still do it on $300 a month, unless you have less than 40 working years ahead of you. If so, you will have to save more so you can get there faster.

In the absence of clearly defined goals, we are forced to concentrate on activity and ultimately become enslaved by it. If the goals were taken out of basketball, a bunch of people would aimlessly be running up and down the floor dribbling a ball. Who would want to watch that? Who would want to *do* that? If the goal posts and end zones were taken off football fields, the Lombardi Trophy would go to the team with the nicest legs. If the goals were taken out of hockey you'd have 12 guys on the ice fighting. Some people think that would improve the sport.

If the goals were absent in any sport, the most significant aspect of recreational pursuit would be removed -- goal setting and striving. There is something inherent that makes us want to do something better, faster, higher, shorter, longer to win. And when it comes to the accumulation and preservation of wealth, the same goal setting principles apply.

Chequemate

But you say it's fun to score touchdowns and shoot baskets, but it isn't fun -- in fact it's downright hard -- to put $300 a month into a savings account. Nobody ever said goal striving is supposed to be easy. In fact, if it's too easy, it's not fun.

What would happen if the Dallas Cowboys showed up for a Super Bowl game and there was no opponent? Who would sit around for 60 minutes watching Emmett Smith score touchdowns if no one was trying to tackle him? How fun would it be to watch Michael Jordan shoot baskets if three guys weren't trying to stop him?

There's a price to pay if you want to achieve significant financial goals. But if you think it's too hard and requires too much effort to build a million-dollar nest egg, think how tough it will be if you remain on the interest-debt treadmill and have no pension when you retire. General George S. Patton said, *"A pint of sweat today will save a gallon of blood tomorrow."*

Scott Peck began his best selling book, *The Road Less Traveled,* saying, *"Life is difficult. This is a great truth, one of the greatest truths. It is a great truth because once we truly see this truth, we transcend it. Once we truly understand and accept it -- then life is no longer difficult. Because once it is accepted, the fact that life is difficult no longer matters."*

This book is not a get-rich-quick panacea, but a guide to spending money in such a way as to achieve worthy financial goals.

Following are some time-tested guidelines for setting and achieving worthwhile goals, from *The Game of Work* by Chuck Coonradt.

Goals must be written. Some people say they can remember their goals without writing them down, but if their spouse calls and asks them to stop at the store, on the way home, and pick up five things, they automatically reach for a piece of paper to write down the five items so they won't forget.

Goals not written down are wishes. Goals not written

down are easily forgotten or changed. Written goals which are internalized, by regular review, become reality.

Many people resist writing down goals. They must think the Dallas Cowboys make up their plays in the huddle. One of the main differences between professional and sandlot football is the amount of written documentation for achieving goals.

A good team doesn't just set goals to win or to be the best. Good goal programs are detailed and specific -- yards per carry, number of offensive and defensive plays, plays per series, etc. Major goals are usually supported by a greater number of sub targets. Achieving sub targets helps you reach the final goal.

We need written goals in managing money. None of us would build a $300,000 home without a set of plans. What would you think if your builder said, "We don't need plans. I've got a pretty good idea what kind of house you want. Let's break ground in the morning."

But an income earner producing $30,000 a year for 10 years, a total of $300,000, will spend every penny without a set of plans or goals. Then at the end of ten years, he will wonder why he has nothing more than the appreciation in his house.

Goals must be your own. You no doubt have observed people who go through life giving the minimum daily requirement at work. Yet when the whistle blows, they are off to coach a little league team, play in a bowling league, build a mountain cabin --do something they enjoy. You've noticed the transformation, the new energy, the intelligence, the creativity, the increased endurance and capacity for work they have when they are doing things which interest them.

Nobody can set your financial goals for you. If you are going to be doing all of the work to achieve your goals, they need to be your own personal goals, no one else's. Mary directed me in setting goals, but in the end, they were my goals not hers.

Goals must be positive. Vince Lombardi said the objective of football is to win -- fairly, squarely and by the rules, but to win. The goal in sports is not to avoid a loss or defeat.

Chequemate

How many times have you seen a PGA golfer going down the stretch suddenly change his game plan to see his lead slip away? He is beaten because he loses the momentum of his earlier, positive attack.

Possibly the most common goal in America is to lose weight. Sometimes we feel it would be easier to cut off an arm than diet to lose 20 pounds. Instead of having a negative goal measured in pounds, it is better to set a positive goal to achieve an optimal weight and maintain that weight once achieved.

One of the problems with losing weight is that we, more often than not, gain it back again and perhaps more. There are several reasons for this, including negative feelings and thoughts associated with taking off unwanted pounds. Negative goals are not pleasant to visualize, so the tendency is to avoid them, forget them. Do you want to be thinking about bankruptcy all the time, if your financial goal is to avoid it? Does it sound fun to constantly think about budgeting, belt-tightening and deprivation? It is much more pleasant to visualize how contented we will be when we have no debt, how much fun it will be to get a call from our stock broker saying our $600,000 pension fund earned another $75,000 last year. Think how proud you will feel when you write out a check for $10,000 to cover the first year's tuition when your child gets accepted to college.

In basketball and football they count the points you score, not the ones you miss. Financial goals should be that way too.

Goals must be measurable and specific. In sports we demand numbers, sometimes two or three places to the right of the decimal point. The times of swimmers, speed skaters and downhill skiers are all measured in thousandths of seconds, and in order to separate one athlete from the other, these exact measurements are essential.

How much, how many, and by when? If you can't measure it, how will you know when you achieve it? Even intangible goals need tangible indicators. If you have a goal to be more patient, count how many times you spank or yell at your children in a month. If the numbers drop, you know your patience is increasing. Don't say, "I am going to be a better salesman next year." Instead, write down how many sales calls you are going to make.

If you put a hundred people in a room and ask them how many would like to be financially independent, all of the hands will go up. Then if you ask how many have a current financial statement listing all of their assets and liabilities, no more than ten hands will go up. It's hard to get where you want to be if you don't know where you are right now. A saying at IBM states, *you get better results from what you **inspect** than what you **expect**.*

Now, if you ask how many in the group have projections of what they want their financial statement to look like in five, ten, fifteen or twenty years, maybe one hand will go up, and that person will become your millionaire. It doesn't make any difference what his or her background is, how much money he or she has, or what his or her current income is. That individual has a plan, and with that plan, you cannot turn him or her aside. Goals must answer the question how much, how many and by when.

Goals must be stated in the most visible terms available. When goals are measured in real terms, everybody knows the score. It's harder to rationalize, fudge and cheat. There's no monkey business. When the points are displayed on the scoreboard, everybody knows what is happening, who is ahead and who is catching up or widening the lead.

Instead of setting a goal to become a millionaire, set a goal to be completely out of debt by a specific time, have X dollars in your pension fund by a certain date. Be able to pay cash for that new Dodge truck by a certain date, or be able to pay for that European vacation by the summer of a certain year.

Goals must contain a deadline. If you don't have a deadline, you don't have a goal. Goals must include how much and *by when.* The most exciting play in all sports occurs in the last two minutes of the half and before the end of the game.

Deadlines allow the student who has slept in all semester to stay up all night studying for the final exam. Because of deadlines in telethons, 40% of the money is raised in the last 20% of the time. One of Murphy's laws states, *The first 10% of the work consumes 90% of the time allowed for the job. The second 90% requires 90% of the time too, and that's why jobs take twice as long to finish.*

Deadlines are the foundation of commitment. Deadlines are the adrenaline boosters. Deadlines are the instigators of achievement and inventiveness. A person four years from retirement has a lot more motivation to save than a person 40 years from retirement. A goals program without deadlines is merely a philosophical statement.

Goals must contain personality changes. The reason many of us don't earn more money is that we wouldn't know what to do with it if we had it. Too frequently, poor people have poor ways, not just in managing their money, but in managing their lives. If your office, house and garage are messy, your finances will be that way too. If you're too lazy to get out of bed in the morning, you'll be too lazy to maintain a disciplined financial management program.

Mary had me read a book by J. Paul Getty. The title was *Being Rich.* Not *Getting Rich,* but *Being Rich.* He talked about responsibilities associated with having wealth and the personality traits necessary to develop and manage wealth. Paul Meyer said, *"You must first set goals to become before you set goals to have."*

Goals are the intangible characteristics that make winners who they are. You cannot become a great downhill skier if you are afraid of personal injury. *You cannot live on 90% of your income if you are frantic to keep up with the Joneses.*

If you take an average individual in an average job earning an average income, you can guess that person will never get ahead as long as things stay the same. But, put that person in a traumatic situation, maybe a costly divorce or a major medical operation, and that person will rise to the occasion and generate an increased income; or he'll fall back into the role of a loser and look to someone else or the government to meet his obligations. We shouldn't wait for a life tragedy to make us change, we can use target setting and goal striving to change on our own. *By setting and achieving personal targets, we can change by choice.*

Goals work better if they contain benefits and rewards. A good idea in setting goals is to establish an arbitrary reward when the goal is accomplished. When all the debts are paid off, or perhaps just the house mortgage, treat yourself and your family to that great vacation in the south seas. When all the VISA cards are paid off, treat yourself and your spouse to a lobster dinner --but don't use the VISA card to pay for it. Wouldn't it be better to buy a new suit as a reward for paying off the home equity loan instead of buying one because somebody decided to put the suits on sale? Every time you and your spouse get through another month of living on 90% of your income, treat yourselves to dinner and a movie in the city.

Goals must be realistic and obtainable. A yard here, a yard there. Woody Hays, one of the great legends in college football, is synonymous with "three yards and a cloud of dust." With that concept, Woody dominated Big 10 football for decades. The three-yards-and-a-cloud-of-dust attitude will get you closer to your financial goals than any instant accomplishments or get-rich-quick schemes.

Financial Goals
Identify your six most important goals.

__Become debt free.

__Retire early with financial security.

__Buy/pay off a home.

__Establish an emergency fund.

__Reduce financial stress

__Gain control of finances.
__Reduce taxes
__Own a business.
__Have money for a dream vacation.
__Own a better car, free and clear.
__Be able to fund college educations for children.
__Help children with down payments for first homes.
__Own a farm or a mountain cabin.
__Own a motor home.
__Build a swimming pool and spa.
__Other_____

In the space provided below write down your financial goals in order of importance, including the amount of money needed to accomplish each goal by each target completion date:

Goal	Amount	Target Date
1.		
2.		
3.		
4.		
5.		
6.		

Just remember, that even though there may be things in life more important to you than financial goals -- lasting marriages, happy children, fulfilling careers, humanitarian service projects --your ability to function in the more important areas of life is greatly influenced by your financial stability. If financial worries are causing heart palpitations and high blood pressure, you are less likely to help your new neighbors unload the moving van. If you can't pay your phone bill, you are less likely to drop everything and drive to Alabama to help flood victims. How would you feel if the doctor said you needed to move your spouse to a milder climate, but you couldn't afford to quit your job, without crippling yourself financially? Having financial order and control in your life lays a foundation that enables you to devote more time, energy, creativity, and money to family, hobbies, even community or humanitarian service.

Mary reminded me from time to time that what we were doing was not about the love of money, but the love of life; about a better life available to anyone willing to change spending habits in order to achieve worthy financial goals. *The amount of time you spend worrying about money is in reverse proportion to how well you manage your money.* If you don't like worrying about money, apply the principles in this book so you won't have to spend so much time fretting over financial problems.

When I had learned everything I could about targets, I returned to Mary for another game of chess, and instruction on the third law.

Targeting -- The second law of debt-free prosperity.

That which each of us calls our 'necessary expenses' will always grow to equal our income unless we protest to the contrary.
--George Clason

The Third Law

T he next time I went to see Mary I figured I knew everything there was to know about goals, and was ready for the third law. As soon as she invited me in I asked her to tell me about the third law. Without responding immediately to my question, she went to the kitchen and fixed us each a cold drink. As she returned to her place at the sofa, she had that look in her eye like she was sizing me up again, trying to decide how much I was ready to receive.

"In order for your goals to become reality, you need a plan to follow in achieving them. You can't put a realistic plan in place without understanding the third law, so I probably shouldn't make you wait any longer."

"Good," I said, "I'm listening."

"You'll find the money to fund your goals by living on less than you earn. *The third law is: live on less than you earn so you can have a surplus to get you out of debt and invest in assets that appreciate.*"

"With two teenagers and a busy wife, there is no surplus at my house," I said. "There is never anything left over at the end of the month. Even with all the tracking, I am barely able to pay my bills. I don't know how we could spend any less."

"The third law doesn't say you have to spend less, just spend differently. *You pay yourself first, instead of last.* You don't wait until the end of the month to see if anything is left over for yourself. You pay yourself first, then make yourself live on what's left for the remainder of the month. *The key to having a surplus for your financial goals is to pay yourself first, and then live on what's left over."*

"That doesn't sound easy."

"It can be, but who said life is supposed to be easy? *No one, regardless of income, can be financially successful unless they live on less than they earn.* The third law is absolutely essential. I call it trimming."

"I don't know if I can do it," I said.

"There's someone I want you to meet," she said. "Julio," she called, turning her head towards the back of the house. A minute later, her gardener entered the room, a handsome young man, perhaps in his early thirties.

"Julio," she said to him. "I know this request is somewhat personal, but I would like you to show Paul your bank book."

"No problem," Julio said, with a strong accent. He removed a tiny bank book from his shirt pocket and handed it to me.

There were lots of pages of transactions, only deposits, and the amounts were all the same. $500. Julio had been depositing $500 a month for what seemed years. The balance in the account was just under $20,000. I handed the book back to Julio. Mary thanked him, and told him he could return to his work.

"Julio earns $700 a month and saves $500," she said. "You earn five times as much and can't save anything. You ought to be ashamed of yourself."

"He doesn't have a wife and two children," I protested.

"He has a wife and four children," Mary said. "He sends

them a hundred, he keeps a hundred, and saves the rest. I give him room and board in addition to his salary. Otherwise he couldn't save so much."

"Why does he do it?" I asked.

"He is saving so he can pay cash for a good used school bus. When he returns to his home in central Mexico, the bus will support him and his family. He will be financially independent because he is able to live on less than he earns. You must do the same, but it will be much easier for you."

"How much must I cut our living expenses?" I asked, still not sure it was even possible.

"All three of your financial goals are easily within reach if you can trim your living expenses to 90% of your income."

"I don't see how living on 90% of my income will get me out of debt in five years," I said.

She handed me another piece of paper and asked me to write down all of my debts, the interest I was being charged on each, the monthly payment, and the balance remaining. It wasn't long until I had the entire page filled with numbers. Then, on another piece of paper she had me list the debts in order, starting with the one with the lowest balance.

Then she asked me how long it would take to pay off the smallest debt if I applied the extra $300 a month generated by our trimming. It was a VISA card, and I told her I would have it paid off in less than three months.

Then she asked how long after that it would take to pay off the next debt, another VISA card, if I added the extra $300 to the regular payment, plus the payment I had been making on the retired first debt.

"Two months," I said. We continued this process, eventually using up five sheets of paper. Each time a debt was paid off, we added its payment to the accelerated payment on the next debt. By the time we got to the last debt, the house mortgage, I was making nearly triple payments. If my calculations were correct, and I had to do a little guessing, all of my debts, including the house mortgage, would be paid off in four and a half years.

I went over the numbers a second time, thinking I must have made a mistake. I realized I had probably been too conservative the first time. If I followed this payment schedule, I would be out of debt in about four years. I could feel chills in the back of my neck, and a tear pushing its way into my eye. It had never occurred to me that anything like this was even possible.

But the key was trimming, finding that extra $300 a month, and keeping the monthly payments at the same level, even after debts were eliminated. I still wasn't sure I could do it.

"Why don't you give me a debt consolidation loan?" I asked. "Then it would be easier. I could use your money to pay off all the loans costing more than 8%."

"We have an agreement," she reminded me. "First you must demonstrate your ability to live the laws. Your tracking is coming along fine. You have written down some worthy targets. Now you have to trim your living expenses to 90% of your income. It is time for Paul Smith to become a little bit like Julio. Remember, there is only one more law after you master trimming, then you will have access to $2,000,000."

After returning home, I stayed up until 2 a.m. poring over canceled checks, bills, and my tracking records. I was determined to find an extra $300 for my debt elimination program, but I still didn't know where it would come from. I had already cut back the video rentals and eliminated the overdraft charges.

The first big breakthrough came when I was looking at my bank statement. The previous month I had noticed and eliminated the overdraft charges. Now I discovered additional charges for things like "analysis," check printing, and "service." Looking at my wife's statements, I found similar charges. Together we were paying about $50 a month for the convenience of checking. Judy and I talked about it, and closed both accounts.

The Third Law

We decided to go without checking accounts until we had enough savings to qualify for those free checking accounts.

We canceled our cable television service. Judy decided she could do her own nails, and she started cutting Billy's hair. Mine, too.

Looking at the itemized charges on the phone bill, I discovered we were paying close to $30 a month for things like call forwarding, call waiting, and some other service that would give us the phone numbers of all the people who had called while we were gone. I called the phone company and canceled those services.

In going over the long distance calls, I discovered Judy enjoyed frequent and lengthy telephone conversations with her mother in California, during work days when rates are highest. I persuaded her to save us another $10 a month by calling her mother nights and weekends.

I cut our video rentals even more when I discovered videos could be checked out free at the library. When I pushed for this change, my wife reminded me about all the money I spent on books to read on my road trips. She said I could save another $20 a month, if I checked books out of the library before my trips. I agreed.

Catching the spirit of what we were doing, Judy offered to wash my shirts and her blouses, instead of sending them to the laundry, if I would do the dinner dishes three nights a week. I agreed.

I turned the water heater down from 160 degrees to 140. The gas company said that would save us at least $10 a month. Billy and Lisa agreed to buy discount clothes when I told them I was working on a program to pay their college tuition.

We cleaned out the basement and donated $3,000 worth of items to Goodwill, a deduction that would save about $800 at tax time, or about $60 a month for a year. I didn't replace the chopped-up Christmas tree.

With the arrival of good weather, instead of going out to

dinner every week, Judy and I started going on picnics. It was less expensive than going to restaurants, and a lot more romantic. We saved about $30 a month.

Once I got everyone tracking, the big surprise was approximately $250 a month we were spending on lunches and fast food. The only way I could get everyone to agree to cut this back to $100 a month was to promise to make tuna fish or peanut butter and jelly sandwiches for myself when I was working at home, and eat soft pretzels, corn nuts and apples for lunch when I was on the road.

One nice side benefit of those first two months was losing about 10 pounds. I felt so good I started jogging -- in the streets, of course. I didn't want to pay for a membership in a health spa.

The key to living on less than you earn, is to pay yourself first, as soon as you get your paycheck, and then live on what's left over. Those who wait until the end of the month to see if anything is left over before paying themselves never have any extra money for their financial goals. By default, they have decided to help the doctor make his Mercedes payment rather than fund their own retirement fund.

Everyone should ask, "Who are the most important people in my life?" If it's you and your loved ones, then maybe it's time to take a hard look at a spending program that is keeping the stock holders at your local bank and Eddie Bauer happy, but is doing nothing to get you and your family any closer to your financial goals.

During the early part of your financial program, when you are paying off debts, it may not seem that you are paying yourself first. After all, the excess money is going to creditors, and you will never see it again.

You must look at accelerated debt payments as a process to prevent future interest burdens. *If you pay off a $100,000 house mortgage in 15 years instead of 30, you will save $92,136 in interest payments.*

You must also realize it doesn't make economic sense to

put your money into a 4% certificate of deposit when you are paying the equivalent of 25% interest on outstanding charge card balances. It doesn't make sense to buy into a mutual fund that averages an 8% return when the outstanding balance on your two car loans is costing you 14 %.

As a general rule, the interest you pay when you are in debt is higher than the interest you will earn when you are out of debt and investing money. Therefore, it makes sense to get out of debt before you start investing. Just remember, the sooner you get out of debt, the sooner you will be able to put your money to work earning interest. *Accelerated debt payments are the best way to pay yourself first when you start a financial program.*

After you make the decision to pay yourself first, the next step is to tear up the charge cards and stop buying things that you can't pay for with cash. It's hard to pay off the balance on a charge card if you keep using it. If you can muster the will power to pay yourself first and get rid of your cards, assuming your financial situation is otherwise fairly normal, you can get out of debt in about five years, including paying off your home.

Some people have a hard time understanding that trimming is not an end to spending, but redirecting the way you spend. In applying the four laws, you become a power spender, realizing the most efficient use of your money in achieving financial goals.

Once a person has initiated a tracking process so every dollar is accounted for, set his or her financial goals, and trimmed away the fat in an effort to re-direct those dollars towards achieving appropriate financial goals -- then that person usually becomes more motivated than ever to increase earnings. The individual realizes, "Hey, if I had another $300 a month coming in, I would be out of debt in half the time. I would be a millionaire by age 55, and could retire ten years early. Wow! Where can I find another $300 a month? But if I could figure out a way to earn another $600 a month..."

Chequemate

When first confronted with the challenge of finding additional money to fund financial goals, most people think the money simply isn't there. We can't take lunch money from the kids, or gas money from Dad. We can't sell the house in the suburbs and move into an apartment in the city where the children will join gangs. We don't want to be so cheap that we put nickels instead of dollars on the collection plate at church, or take the dog to the pound so we won't have to buy any more dog food.

What people don't realize is that the simple process of tracking expenses, discussed in this book, will help them find extra money they didn't even know existed, like the man who discovered he was paying premiums on two health insurance policies. He found an extra $200 a month without having to give up anything. What about the small businessman who started tracking every dollar only to discover at tax time he had an extra $3,000 in deductions? If he's in the 30% tax bracket, those additional deductions saved him a thousand dollars, almost a hundred a month. Still, nobody has had to do any belt-tightening.

And who says belt tightening is always bad? Suppose an individual, after a few months of detailed tracking, discovers he and his wife are spending nearly a $100 a month on fountain drinks, and another $100 on alcoholic beverages. Neither one had any idea they were spending and consuming so much. They are faced with the hard truth that maybe they won't even be around to enjoy retirement if they continue filling their bodies with so much sugar, carbonation and alcohol. Strictly for health reasons, they decide to cut these expenses down to $50 a month, and bingo, they have an extra $150 a month, almost enough by itself to fund their retirement program.

Then there's the busy couple like Judy and me, who are concerned about the sub-average report cards of their two teenage children. While tracking family expenses, they realize they are spending $150 a month on cable television and video rentals, and neither one of the parents watches more than three or four hours of television a month. Perhaps if this expense were eliminated, or drastically reduced to about $25 a month, it would be easier to get the children to read and do homework. How much would that $125 a month become in ten years if it were invested at 8% in a college education fund for the children? $22,868. The children might call such a cut severe belt tightening, unnecessary deprivation, or downright child abuse, but try to find a professional educator or counselor who would not applaud such a move.

Present value tables are a wonderful motivation when you start to trim. These tables tell you what the $5 you saved by bringing your lunch to work will be worth when you retire. If you decide to buy $2,000 worth of mutual funds instead of a snowmobile, these tables will tell you how much it will appreciate by the time your children start college, or when you retire. The table below shows how different amounts of money invested monthly at 15% by people of various ages will grow over time into $1-3 million nest eggs.

Save to Become a Millionaire*

Starting Age	Years to age 65	$1 Million	$2 Million	$3 Million
15	50	$7	$14	$20
20	45	15	30	45
25	40	30	60	90
30	35	70	140	210
35	30	150	300	450
40	25	300	600	900
45	20	650	1,300	1,950
50	15	1,500	3,000	4,500
55	10	3,500	7,000	10,500

*Approximate monthly amount to be invested at 15% to produce $1-3 Million by age 65.

Chequemate

Once your tracking program is in place, the first and obvious trimming is getting rid of the waste and unwanted spending, like some of the items mentioned earlier. Then, you take a hard look at your goals, where you want to be, and where you are now. You measure your current net worth (assets less liabilities) and subtract that amount from the net worth you would like to achieve, possibly at retirement. Divide this amount by the number of years until retirement, and you have a pretty good idea how much trimming you are going to have to do. Keep in mind that as you get closer to your goal, your assets are not only appreciating, but are producing income to buy additional assets, a process called compounding. In other words, once you get out of debt and start earning interest, time becomes your friend. A 25-year-old who bites the bullet and saves $500 a month until he is 35, then decides he is tired of saving, and never puts away another nickel the rest of his life, if he never spends the money he saves, and it continues to appreciate at 8% per year, at age 65 he will have $1,000,324.

On the other hand, if a 55-year-old worker who has never saved anything decides to get serious about retirement, and starts saving $500 a month which he invests at 8% ten years later at 65 he will have $91,473.

Both of the above people saved $500 a month for ten years. Both earned an increase of 8% on their savings. Yet the young person earned $908,851 more than the older person. The difference is time. The sooner you start on a savings and investment program, the better. *It is better to save now and play later, than to play now and save later.* Time is money, and the sooner you get it working for you, the better.

If you are already 50 or 55, don't assume it's too late for you to take control of your finances. If you start putting $500 a month into a 15% mutual fund at age 50, you will have $334,253 when you retire. That's a lot more than if you didn't start saving at age 50.

The Third Law

People who are in control of their money have the capacity to be more charitable. *Those in control are the most charitable. Those who are the most charitable are most liked. Those who are most liked are the most successful because everyone wants them to succeed.*

The key to any kind of financial success is learning to live on less than you earn, thereby creating a surplus to invest in assets that earn interest or increase in value. Trimming is the process by which we do this. But no matter how good we are at trimming, it never seems to work if we wait until the end of the month to see how much is left over to invest. Pay yourself first, not last. As soon as you get your paycheck, take the 5%, 10% or 15% you have identified as surplus to reduce debt and buy investments, and take that out first, forcing yourself to live on what's left over.

Most people who do this say they hardly notice any difference in their lifestyle. The tracking process alone can usually uncover enough inefficient spending and downright waste to more than cover a 10% debt-elimination and savings program.

Most Americans, if they start early enough, can achieve financial security on a 10% savings program. If their goals are more aggressive, or if they don't start until later in life, 10% will not be enough. But, before you determine how much surplus you have to create, you must first figure out where you are, where you want to be, and how many years you have to get there. These numbers will give you a pretty good idea where you have to start.

At first I didn't believe Mary when she told me that after trimming my living expenses to the 90% level, I wouldn't miss that extra 10%. She said I might even want to start saving more than that -- maybe 15% or 20%. She said if I would sit down and figure out how much quicker my financial goals could be realized with that increased payment, the idea of cutting living expenses even more would be very attractive.

Chequemate

She said it is important that you look at the amount you are saving not as a sacrifice, but as a payment to yourself to help achieve your most desired financial goals. The third law is about paying yourself first and then living on what's left over.

Trimming -- The third law of debt-free prosperity

The only thing worse than investing in things that depreciate
is paying interest on money invested in things that depreciate.
--Blaine Harris

Debt-Free

The next time I visited Mary I had high hopes of learning the
fourth and final law. But as we sat down for what I thought
was our final game of chess, she wanted to talk about
something else. Debt.

"Have you ever wondered why most American families
who earn as much as you do seem to be struggling financially,
when most of the families of the world live on less than $200 a
month?" she asked. I didn't say anything.

"You nod with understanding when you see the financial
struggle of a factory worker earning $8 an hour," she continued,
"but you shake your head in amazement when a medical doctor
with a guaranteed six-figure income declares bankruptcy.

"There was a time in this country when the person who
spent all of his or her income without saving anything was
considered foolhardy," she added. "Today, the person who
spends all that he earns is only less foolhardy than the millions
who spend more than they earn -- thanks to easy credit. Why is

57

it that the people in the richest nation in the world feel the poorest?"

"I don't know," I responded.

"Because they don't know how to manage their money. People don't seem to stop and wonder how a worker from Mexico or Peru with a green card can support his immediate and extended families on $4 an hour, yet a California family earning $30,000 a year, is never more than a month or two from bankruptcy court."

She went on to explain that not only do we earn more than most of our world neighbors, but we worry more, too. Worrying about money lowers the quality of life, and causes health problems. Financial problems cause 89% of our divorces.

Part of the problem is the quality and quantity of advertising to which we are exposed. Every day we are bombarded with advertisements for home equity loans. "We'll help you get the money out of your house so you can use it." "Home equity debt consolidation makes sense." Every day we get mailers offering new credit cards, some where our credit is guaranteed. Our children start getting these mailers when they are seniors in high school from companies trying to lure them into the interest trap before they know better.

Every one of these ads, just like every cigarette pack, should carry a warning that consumer debt is dangerous to your health, your marriage, and the overall quality of your life. The home equity ads convey the feeling that consumer debt is a warm, fuzzy blanket that will make you feel better, and give you peace of mind. Nothing could be further from the truth.

She said there ought to be an advertisement in which consumer debts are depicted as hairy, black, red-eyed monkeys -- infested with lice and ticks, who leap on your back, dig in with sharp, dirty claws, and refuse to let go your entire adult life unless you take drastic measures to get rid of them.

The first step towards financial peace of mind, if you are

sick and tired of that trapped feeling, is to make the decision to do something, to take the no-debt pledge. I told Mary I had done that.

Mary said you must set your standard of living lower than your level of income, while many of your neighbors and friends set their standard of living at the limit of their credit-worthiness. Mary said she knew a Vietnamese couple who lived on *20%* of their income while saving up to buy their first restaurant. Most of us can get out of debt and achieve financial security by learning to live on *90%* of our income.

Once you start living on less than you earn, you use the excess, or the amount you pay to yourself, to accelerate debt payments and then to build wealth.

If you don't like living on less than you earn, and you don't want to give up the vacation home in Phoenix, even though you earn only $8 an hour, then you ought to seriously look at increasing your income.

You can literally spend your way to wealth. Some people falsely associate the word spend with waste or squander. To spend is to allocate. We all have resources that need to be allocated -- like time and money. How we manage the allocation of these resources determines the quality of our future.

Even though we must learn to live on less than we earn, we still spend all that we earn. With a good financial plan, we don't spend less, we spend differently. We direct our money into channels that get us out of debt and build financial security. Instead of spending our way into a deeper and deeper hole, we spend our way to happiness and security. Other people do it, and so can we.

Mary said about anyone could get out of debt in almost five years without increasing income. Many people don't believe this is possible.

Following is a case study of John and Jill Sample, who planned to have their $31,131 in consumer debt paid off in six years, making regular payments which included $8,284 in interest. While using the debt-eliminator program outlined at the end of this chapter, they were able to pay off their debts in three years and two months, paying $6,888 in interest. By adding another $100 a month, they could have been out of debt in two years and eight months, and saved another $700 in interest.

The key to making a debt-eliminator program work is to keep the dollar amount of monthly payments at the same level as debts are retired. For example, when Sample's VISA card was paid off, they took the $68 a month they had been sending to VISA, and applied it to the next targeted debt, thus accelerating its pay-down time.

Let's assume that after paying off all their debts, using the $100 accelerator, the Samples continued making the same payment into a 12% investment fund. By the time six years passes, the time they targeted originally to get out of debt, instead of just being out of debt, they have $51,467 in their investment fund. In other words, by using the principles taught in this book, in six short years, the Samples went from $31,131 in the red to $51,467 in the black, an $82,598 improvement in their financial net worth!

The first chart gives a breakdown of each of the Sample debts including balances owed, interest rates, monthly minimum payments, number of payments remaining, and real debt, which is the sum of the remaining payments, including principle and interest. The first chart also shows how long it will take the Samples to get out of debt on their current course on the Eliminator plan, or the Eliminator plan plus $100, and how the Eliminator plan plus $100 can not only pay off the debts, but give them $51,467 in savings at the end of six years.

Debt-Free

DEBT ELIMINATOR
Prepared for
John and Jill Sample

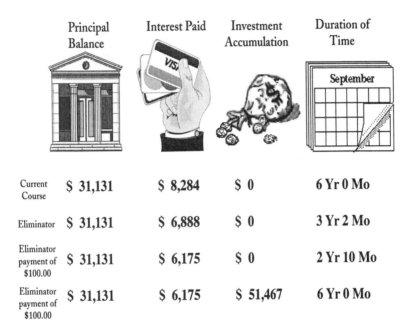

	Principal Balance	Interest Paid	Investment Accumulation	Duration of Time
Current Course	$ 31,131	$ 8,284	$ 0	6 Yr 0 Mo
Eliminator	$ 31,131	$ 6,888	$ 0	3 Yr 2 Mo
Eliminator payment of $100.00	$ 31,131	$ 6,175	$ 0	2 Yr 10 Mo
Eliminator payment of $100.00	$ 31,131	$ 6,175	$ 51,467	6 Yr 0 Mo

Based on these Assumptions: 12.00% Annualized return on investments

Description	Interest Rate	Amount Left	Minimum Payment	Payments Left	Real Debt
Dentist	18.00%	485.00	30.00	19	560
Auto I	7.50%	3,325.00	190.0	19	3,532
Auto II	9.00%	8,800.00	310.00	33	9,932
Home Equity Loan	11.00%	12,000.00	320.00	47	14,772
Discover Card	19.50%	1,700.00	49.00	52	2,522
MasterCard	21.00%	1,985.00	53.00	62	3,255
VISA	19.80%	2,836.00	68.00	72	4,842
Total		31,131.00	1,020.00		39,415

Based on total monthly payments of $ 1120.00 ($ 1020.00 current payment + $ 100.00 accelerator).

61

The second Sample chart gives a month-by-month breakdown showing how each debt is systematically eliminated in 33 months using the $100 accelerator. The formula is quite simple. In the month following payoff of the first debt, Sample adds the amount of that payment to the payment on the second debt. When the second debt is paid off, he adds the combined payments he had been making on the two retired debts to the payments on the third debt until it is paid off. He continues the process, keeping the combined total of all payments at $1120 a month until all the debts are paid off in month 33. This is called debt payment compounding.

Before Sample started the Eliminator program he was targeted to be out of debt in six years, or 72 months. When his debts were paid off in the 34th month, if he continues paying the $1120 a month for 38 months to the end of the original six-year period into a 12% growth fund, the compounded value of those payments at the end of the six-year period is $51,467.

DEBT ELIMINATOR
Monthly payments required to meet your target

Month	Dentist	Auto I	Auto II	Home Equity Loan	Discover Card	MasterCard	VISA	
Aug 94	130.00	190.00	310.00	320.00	49.00	53.00	68.00	1,120.00
Sep 94	130.00	190.00	310.00	320.00	49.00	53.00	68.00	1,120.00
Oct 94	130.00	190.00	310.00	320.00	49.00	53.00	68.00	1,120.00
Nov 94	113.94	207.06	310.00	320.00	49.00	53.00	68.00	1,120.00
Dec 94		320.00	310.00	320.00	49.00	53.00	68.00	1,120.00
Jan 95		320.00	310.00	320.00	49.00	53.00	68.00	1,120.00
Feb 95		320.00	310.00	320.00	49.00	53.00	68.00	1,120.00
Mar 95		320.00	310.00	320.00	49.00	53.00	68.00	1,120.00
Apr 95		320.00	310.00	320.00	49.00	53.00	68.00	1,120.00
May 95		320.00	310.00	320.00	49.00	53.00	68.00	1,120.00
Jun 95		320.00	310.00	320.00	49.00	53.00	68.00	1,120.00
Jul 95		320.00	310.00	320.00	49.00	53.00	68.00	1,120.00
Aug 95		143.02	486.98	320.00	49.00	53.00	68.00	1,120.00
Sep 95			630.00	320.00	49.00	53.00	68.00	1,120.00
Oct 95			630.00	320.00	49.00	53.00	68.00	1,120.00
Nov 95			630.00	320.00	49.00	53.00	68.00	1,120.00
Dec 95			630.00	320.00	49.00	53.00	68.00	1,120.00
Jan 96			630.00	320.00	49.00	53.00	68.00	1,120.00
Feb 96			630.00	320.00	49.00	53.00	68.00	1,120.00
Mar 96			630.00	320.00	49.00	53.00	68.00	1,120.00
Apr 96			460.14	489.86	49.00	53.00	68.00	1,120.00
May 96				950.00	49.00	53.00	68.00	1,120.00
Jun 96				950.00	49.00	53.00	68.00	1,120.00
Jul 96				950.00	49.00	53.00	68.00	1,120.00
Aug 96				950.00	49.00	53.00	68.00	1,120.00
Sep 96				950.00	49.00	53.00	68.00	1,120.00
Oct 96				950.00	49.00	53.00	68.00	1,120.00
Nov 96				950.00	49.00	53.00	68.00	1,120.00
Dec 96				950.00	49.00	53.00	68.00	1,120.00
Jan 97				348.91	650.09	53.00	68.00	1,120.00
Feb 97					285.47	766.53	68.00	1,120.00
Mar 97						537.43	582.57	1,120.00
Apr 97							1,120.00	1,120.00
May 97							346.22	346.22

Debt-Free

Now, if you really want to get excited about what a debt-eliminator program can do for you, make a list of your own debts on the table *Debt-Eliminator Work Sheet* . You'll need to know payment amounts, number of payments remaining, interest rates, and approximate balances. Fill in the blanks the best you can. If necessary, call financial institutions for additional information.

Once all the appropriate debt information is recorded in the first table, go to the left hand column of the graph on the following two pages and enter numbers for months (10/96, 11/96, etc.) for 60 consecutive months, starting with the current month. Now, moving horizontally across the top of the graph, write a name to describe each debt (VISA, pickup, home equity, etc.).

Be sure to rank the debts according to the number of payments remaining, starting with the ones with the fewest remaining payments, not the ones with the highest interest rates. The reason for this is to get into a situation where you are making double, triple and quadruple payments as soon as possible. *This gives you the feeling you are exterminating your debts with reckless abandon, a wonderful experience after years of feeling enslaved by them.*

To determine the monthly payment total in the right hand column, just add up all payments on the debts you listed, and add the $100 accelerator. Don't worry about where the extra $100 will come from. Remember, the monthly payment amount in the right hand column must remain the same as the debts are eliminated.

Now, start filling in the columns, one row at a time, from left to right. If you listed the debts in the right order, the debt in the left column will be retired first. When you fill in the next row, take the amount you had been paying on the retired debt, and add it to the payment on the second debt.

At this point, you need to do a little creative arithmetic. Because you have increased the amount of the second payment, you have shortened the payoff time. Divide the new payment into the approximate balance, plus some estimated interest to determine how many months it will take to retire that debt. Continue filling in all the blanks, a row at a time, until the second debt is retired. Then add this payment to the payment of the third debt. Continue this process until all of the debts are eliminated.

Most people, when they are finished filling in the blanks, think they have made a mistake, because the amount of time required to get out of debt is much shorter than they at first guessed. Some people stand up and shout, "I can do this!" or "Why didn't I do this ten years ago?"

Itemized Debts

	Debt 1	Debt 2	Debt 3	Debt 4	Debt 5	Debt 6
Balance						
Payment						
Interest						
# Pmts.						

Debt-Free

Debt Eliminator Work Sheet

	Debt 1	Debt 2	Debt 3	Debt 4	Debt 5	Debt 6	Pmts.
Month							
(10/96)							

Chequemate

Debt Eliminator Work Sheet (cont'd)

Month	Debt 1	Debt 2	Debt 3	Debt 4	Debt 5	Debt 6	Pmts.
(10/96)							

Debt-Free

Now, if you really want to get excited, look at the annuity table below and figure what your monthly payment amount from the right hand column of the work sheet will be worth in 5, 10, 15 and 20 years if you pay that amount into a 12% investment fund after all your debts are paid off. See how wonderful it is to have interest working for you instead of against you.

Monthly Investment Annuity Table at 12%

	$500	$600	$700	$800	$900	$1,000	$1,100
5 yrs.	40,835	49,001	57,169	65,336	73,503	81,670	89,837
10 yrs.	115,019	138,023	161,027	184,031	207,035	230,039	253,043
15 yrs.	249,790	299,748	349,706	399,664	449,622	499,580	549,538
20 yrs.	494,628	593,553	692,479	791,404	890,330	989,255	1,088,181

Note: If you are having a difficult time figuring out your own debt elimination plan, as explained in this chapter, Chequemate International will do a confidential analysis for you, for a minimal charge of only $10. Just send in a list of your debts, along with monthly payments of each, interest rates, number of payments remaining, and balances. (Refer to page 68 for a Sample Input Sheet.) Chequemate will enter your information into the computer and send you a printout showing you what you have to do to get out of debt, usually in five years or less. Send the information with a return address and your check to:

Chequemate International
57 West 200 South, Suite 350
Salt Lake City, Utah 84101

Chequemate

DEBT ELIMINATOR
Input Sheet

Client Number: _____

First Name: _____   Last Name: _____   Spouse Name: _____

Address: _____

City St Zip: _____

Extra Cash Applied to Eliminator: _____

Annualized return on investments: _____

Description	Interest Rate	Amount Left	Monthly Payment

The people who understand money spend it on assets that generate wealth. Those who don't understand money, spend it on things that consume wealth, and thus the rich get richer and the poor get poorer.
--Blaine Harris

The Fourth Law

The next time I saw Mary, I had been tracking my expenses for three months and living on less than 90% of my income for two months. I read my goal sheet every night and morning, and three of my five credit cards and the overdraft debt were gone forever.

When I explained all this to Mary, she said I was ready for the fourth law.

"Once you get out of debt," she began, "You don't just squander all that new money you will have by not having to pay interest. You start buying things that appreciate in value. You never stop spending, you just spend differently, more wisely. You have to change. You need to become more interested in mutual funds than convertible sports cars from Italy. We live in a world of money, but managing money can be as complicated and sophisticated as you want to make it. There's much to learn."

"So what is the fourth law?" I asked, wanting her to say it

in a few words.

"First, let's play a little chess," she suggested. I followed her to the chess board. As eager as I was to learn the fourth law, I was more eager to play chess. She had whipped me three times in a row. I was determined to engineer a different outcome this time.

She seemed intent on philosophizing on the fourth law. Good. I encouraged her to talk about that while I concentrated on winning the game.

"Albert Einstein once said the most powerful thing he ever discovered was compound interest," she said.

"Was that before or after he invented the atomic bomb?" I asked. "What do you think he meant?"

"It means a 15-year-old who can start saving $7 a month, and sticks with it, earning a 15% return, can retire with a million dollars," she said emphatically. "It means a young housewife who prepares a few cheap meals a month so she can salt away $25 in a growth mutual fund, if she sticks with it, can accumulate a million dollars. It means Paul Smith can retire with a million dollars if he can live on 90% of what he earns, and invest the difference wisely."

"So what's the fourth law?" I asked, still concentrating on the game.

"About 40 years ago," she continued, ignoring my question, "after I had mastered the first three laws, and had saved a little money to invest, I thought I'd make a killing investing in pork belly futures. I guess I was short on patience, but I was still tracking and trimming. I wanted to make a lot of money fast. Instead, I lost the entire $2,000 I had worked so hard to save. I was devastated. It was like I had lost all the money in the world. I thought I was going to have to take a second job to cover my losses."

"So what did you do?"

"I just continued tracking and trimming, but this time I did something different. As I was building a new nest egg, I started reading investment books and attending seminars. I wasn't about to lose $2,000 that fast a second time. And I didn't. Today my investments earn me over $2,000 a day..."

"Wow," I said, not meaning to interrupt her. But the thought of someone earning $2,000 a day while puttering in the yard and playing chess, couldn't help but trigger a verbal reaction from me.

"I look at that $2,000 loss as the price I had to pay to learn the fourth law, or my tuition," she said. "If you listen closely to what I am saying, you can learn the fourth law for free."

"So what's the fourth law?" I demanded.

"I want you to attend a real estate seminar, and have a real estate professional show you at least one piece of property a week."

"All my money is committed to getting out of debt," I said. "I can't think about buying real estate."

"Nobody said anything about buying, at least not yet. I also want you to attend a stock, bond and securities investment seminar, and read at least two books on the subject."

"I don't have any money to invest in stocks either," I said.

"But you will, so you must get ready now. I want you to read the *Wall Street Journal* and *Money Magazine,* subscribe to an investment newsletter, and find a counselor or money manager who is more interested in a long-term relationship than short-term commissions."

"What is the fourth law?" I asked, thinking if I could stay on this track ten more minutes, I might win the game.

"Success happens when preparation meets opportunity. If you don't prepare you will never be able to seize those wonderful investment opportunities that present themselves every day in the stock market and the world of real estate."

"So the fourth law is preparation?" I asked, thinking I was about three moves from checkmate.

"I call it training, because training fits better with the other three laws -- tracking, targeting and trimming. Now you have it all. *If you steer yourself onto a lifetime course of tracking, targeting, trimming, and training you will never want for the material things in this world.* Now tell me the things I asked you to do to demonstrate your training proficiency."

I couldn't remember any of them except that I was supposed to read the *Wall Street Journal* and *Money Magazine*.

"Maybe I had better get a piece of paper and write them down," I said. "Would you say them again."

"Checkmate," she said after making her last move. I tried not to show my disappointment in losing again. I borrowed a piece of paper from her desk and wrote down the things she wanted me to do to start my own money management training program.

By the time we met again, I had paid off and destroyed all the charge cards and the overdraft balance, attended two investment seminars, read four books, and looked at six pieces of real estate. I was reading the *Wall Street Journal* at work because I couldn't afford a subscription, and talked the library into subscribing to *Money Magazine* so I could drop in once a month and read it.

Mary assured me we were not working on a quick fix for my financial worries. Nor were we talking about a get-rich-quick scheme that requires no effort or risk. She said we were talking about change, a long-term change, developing a different way to look at money, changing the way I thought and acted in money matters, setting financial goals with more emphasis on debt elimination and savings as opposed to getting more things.

"Most of us need to change the way we acquire and keep track of our money," she explained. Most of us need to change the way we budget so we can live on less than we earn. Most of us need to change the way we spend, with more emphasis on buying the things that increase in value.

Many of us carry a lot of emotional baggage which makes these attitude and behavior changes especially difficult. We've inherited attitudes and behavior patterns from our parents. If

The Fourth Law

Mom and Dad kept their financial papers in a box under the bed, we tend to do the same. If Mom grew up in the depression watching her mother hide money in a coffee can, she will probably do it, too. If Dad bought whatever toy he wanted using the "I deserve this" rationale, the son will probably become a spendthrift, too.

A young mother learned she inherited her parents' hand-me-down attitudes about money.

"At 13, I was determined not to do the things my mother did that irritated me. Now I'm 33, and I don't want to pass on to my daughter the thing I like least about my life -- my financial situation.

"My husband, Mark, works hard and is a good father, but we aren't getting along. We have everything we want, just like my Mom and Dad. They had everything but peace of mind, and we're in the same boat.

"Mark wants to budget. Sounds gruesome to me. We need a solution before things get worse. We're so right for each other, and we get along so well. If it weren't for the money problems...

"I just had to have it all, now, just like Mom and Dad. But, now I want so badly to be 'even' financially, that I am buying lottery tickets. I can't pass this on to my daughter.

"As a little girl I cringed when my wardrobe was augmented with 'hand-me-downs.' But now I punish myself because I've taken my parents' hand-me-down financial beliefs and allowed them to hurt me and my family."

It's time to change, if we haven't already. We live in a world that runs on money, so we might as well develop the attitudes and behaviors that will enable us to prosper in a world of money. Whether we like it or not, using money is something everyone has to do. We can use it foolishly and thoughtlessly and become slaves to it, or we can use it wisely, putting it to work for us, not only so we can enjoy the abundance and prosperity of the world, but, also, so we can be more effective in lightening the burdens of others.

Chequemate

I knew a student who wrote on his application for admission to business school that he wanted to learn how to earn and manage money so he would have the freedom in his life to do many things that had nothing to do with money.

The sad truth is those who spurn money, and resist learning how to use it, often end up spending more time worrying about it than those who took the time early on to master the principles involved in acquiring, keeping and managing money.

It is the lack of money, or the lack of ability to manage money, that fills our prisons. The lack of money pushes potentially fine, talented, intelligent people into crimes of theft, murder, prostitution, drugs, and even suicide. It makes people do things they otherwise would never dream of doing.

The people who understand money spend it on assets that generate wealth. Those who don't understand money, spend it on things that consume wealth, and thus the rich get richer and the poor get poorer. By following the principles outlined in this book, you can join the 10% of the people who provide the money for the other 90% to borrow.

Like in most of life's endeavors, basic principles are involved in getting and keeping money. Those principles can be learned in books, classes and seminars, from counselors and advisors, and in the world of hard knocks. Some people claim they have made and lost several fortunes before they learned to preserve wealth.

Nobody has to go back to school, change careers, or buy a seat on the New York stock exchange. Learning about money is like driving a car. You may not aspire to drive in the Indy 500, but if you are to get along in this world, you must have sufficient skill with a car, and sufficient knowledge of traffic laws to get to and from work, and to be able to negotiate your way through a big city, on and off the freeways. You may not want to read the *Wall Street Journal* every day, or go to MBA school, but anyone can subscribe to a financial newsletter, read an occasional money management book, even join an investment club that meets once or twice a month.

The basic principles involved in managing money are presented in this book. Track your daily expenses. Set targets. Live on less than you earn. Pay yourself first. Get out of debt. Get to where you are collecting interest instead of paying it. But there is much more to learn, especially after you get out of debt and are starting to look for places to put your money to work.

For example, one of the most dangerous fallacies among novice investors is that the rate of return is directly related to the amount of risk. The greater the risk, the greater the potential return. Sometimes this is true, but, many times it isn't.

Suppose a marginal friend, who went through bankruptcy several years earlier, comes to you and wants to borrow $50,000. As collateral, he is willing to put up a free-and-clear piece of commercial real estate in the center of your town that he just inherited from the estate of an aunt. He has a recent appraisal on the property showing its value at $875,000. He is so excited about this new inheritance, that he wants to take his wife on a trip around the world. That's why he wants to borrow the $50,000. Because of the embarrassment of bankruptcy, and a potential time problem, he would rather get the money from you than from a bank. He wants to leave on the vacation in the next few days. He is willing to pay you 18% interest on the loan. He will pay you back in a few months, after he decides what he wants to do with the property.

If you had the cash, would you make the loan? Of course. Then you would feel guilty every time you found yourself wishing your friend and his wife would get sidetracked in Borneo and never return. Your risk is almost zero, and the return is five times what you are getting on your savings account at the bank. High return, low risk. Once in a while an opportunity like this comes along. But you can never take advantage of such an opportunity unless you have accumulated some liquid assets. *Success is defined as the place where preparation meets opportunity.*

Is there such a thing as a low-return, high-risk investment? Sure. Suppose the boy next door decides to drop out of school to become a rock star. He asks you to loan him $50,000 so he can buy a new electric guitar, a lizard skin suit, and a van with curtains on the windows so he can take your daughter with him to Los Angeles to make his first record deal. He says he'll pay you a 6% return on your investment, two points better than what you are earning in the savings account. Low return, high risk. And, he's mad when you say, "No".

Suppose a stock broker gets you all excited about buying pork bellies and other commodities on margin. He says a little bit of an upswing in demand can literally double your money overnight.

Tired of the 5% return at the bank, you give him the nest egg you have been feeding $300 a month for ten years, hoping you will double its value in a few days. A week later, when you call the broker, he tells you that instead of taking a gentle upswing, the market took a gentle downswing. Then there is silence on the phone. "What does that mean?" you ask. Then, in a matter-of-fact tone, he tells you all your money is gone. "You lost it all. Do you want to try again?"

Unfortunately, in school people receive more training on how to drive cars than how to handle money. Classes ought to be offered in "Personal Accounting" (tracking), "Financial Strategies" (goal setting), "Budget Reality" (trimming), "Debt Management and Elimination", "Asset Accumulation I, II & III", "Real Estate for Dummies", "Introduction to Offshore Investing", "Asset Management", and "Protecting Your Nest Egg". Each of these subject headings could be a four credit hour course, just for starters. There's plenty to learn, and if you're serious about getting control of your financial life, a certain amount of your time and resources should be allocated to learning.

One dangerous pitfall for new investors is placing too

much value in "hot tips." If you make your stock purchase selections by throwing a dart at a list of Dow Jones stocks, your return will be around 8% because that's how much the Dow Jones average goes up in a typical year. If you make your purchases based on "hot tips" you hear in the gym or cafeteria, you'll probably do worse than 8%. Still, everyone should have a trusted financial counselor. There are too many potential pitfalls, and too much at risk, to make major financial decisions without council you can trust.

The first time you read this book, you might get the impression borrowing is bad. Not always. How many stories have you heard about people borrowing their way into a nice house or a big piece of land, only to see the value double in a few years, sometimes making hundreds of thousands of dollars for the borrower?

Borrowing for a home is one of the best investments anyone can make, but instead of paying it off in 30 years with two-thirds of your payments going to interest, save tens of thousands of dollars by paying it off in 10 or 15 years.

The young people who took out student loans 20 years ago so they could go to college, for the most part are financially better off today than their counterparts who went to work out of high school. A study by the Governmental Commission on Mental Illness and Health concluded that there is a close relationship between years in school and the sense of well-being and satisfaction in life. The perspectives of college graduates were broader and aspiration levels higher. When they worried, their worries tended to be over genuine, not imagined, troubles, but no group escapes stress.

It's OK to borrow for things that increase in value. It's smart to borrow to buy a piece of real estate you think will double in value in two or three years. It's smart to take out a $10,000 home improvement loan if the resulting improvements add $20,000 to the value of your home. It's even smarter to invest in your own future by getting the best education available in your chosen field. If your son or daughter gets an opportunity to go to one of the best universities where the tuition is over $10,000 a year, the family will be money ahead to help him or her do it. Starting salaries for Harvard-trained lawyers average about $80,000 a year. When preparation and opportunity come together, the result is success.

Borrowing for a car can be argued both ways. A car may depreciate in value, but you need reliable transportation to make a living. Just remember, borrowing to buy a good used car so you can get to and from work isn't the same as buying a $45,000 BMW with a 5% down payment.

There's a place in every financial plan where you forget all the talk about positive thinking, and develop a failure avoidance strategy. Ask yourself, "How can I screw up? This is when you realize that one medical disaster in a week could wipe out that $300 a month you have been saving for ten years if you don't have adequate health insurance. This is when you realize that if you suddenly died, before the pension fund is fully funded, your spouse wouldn't have enough to live on if you don't have life insurance. "What if, when I turn 50, they decide to give my job to a woman half my age? Could I reduce the chance of that happening with more training, or should I look at starting a small business on my own before I'm forced to do it?"

If you are paying more than 20% of your income in taxes (the average worker making $40,000 with two children and a mortgage pays 30% of his income in direct and indirect taxes), you might want to start looking at small or home business opportunities. An immediate benefit of such a business is another eight to ten thousand dollars in legitimate tax deductions.

The ultimate small business for tax benefits is the small ranch or farm with at least one hired man. First of all you, don't pay sales tax on anything you buy because you are producing food for resale. You can deduct gasoline and diesel, food, utilities, and lots of fun toys. You need a four-wheeler to check the irrigation, snowmobiles to check the cattle, guns and ammo to keep the predators away, airplanes to find lost livestock, computers to keep up with commodity prices, and you must attend the farm and ranch conventions in Hawaii every winter -- all tax deductible expenses. The only problem is the price of six-month-old calves has dropped from a $1.10 a pound to $.55 a pound since N.A.F.T.A. was passed by Congress.

"If you are serious about preserving money, financial education and training should be an ongoing part of your financial strategy," Mary advised as she won another game of chess.

Training -- The fourth law of debt-free prosperity

We firmly believe the strength and prosperity of a nation or society depends largely on the strength and prosperity of its families.
--Blaine Harris

Tables Turned

I was on the road a lot that spring, and didn't see Mary again until the charge cards were paid off and destroyed. After months of tracking, it was automatic, and we no longer missed the things we had trimmed out of our budget. I remembered Mary saying that *while it may be possible to have anything you need, you can't have everything you want.*

One evening when Mary and I got together for chess, I told her that when real estate agents tried to qualify me by asking how much money I had to invest, I told them I had a $2,000,000 line of credit.

"I guess you do," she said. "As far as I am concerned you have satisfied your part of the agreement. How much of the $2,000,000 do you want?"

"Maybe we better discuss it over a game of chess," I suggested. I didn't tell her I had read a book titled *Winning Chess Strategies* along with all the investment and real estate books.

While we were playing, I told her about the debts Judy and I had retired, and that we were now working on the home equity loan which was at 8 ½%. Thanks to a couple of nice real estate commissions Judy had received, we were ahead of schedule on our debt elimination plan. I told Mary that since my first mortgage was 7 ½%, I didn't really need any of the 8% money in the $2,000,000 line of credit.

"Are you telling me you don't want my money, after all you've gone through to get approved?" She sounded surprised, shocked, even hurt.

"I'm not telling you I don't want it. I just don't need it now. My first financial goal is to get out of debt. Why would I want to incur more debt? Why would I want to go deeper in debt if I am on target to be out of debt completely in less than four years?"

"Maybe you'll need some help getting into a piece of real estate where you think you can double your money," she offered.

"In that event, I'll be knocking at your door asking for some of that 8% money," I said. Then I hesitated. I stood up, and motioned for her to stand up too.

"I'm already so much in debt to you," I said as I put my arms around her. Tears were streaming from my eyes as I kissed both of her cheeks. "Thank you so much," I said, finally pushing her back so I could look into her tear-flooded eyes. She didn't say anything, but I could tell from her gentle smile that she was happy, too.

We resumed our game as I told her the story of the man who was walking along the beach at low tide. He noticed thousands of starfish lying on the wet sand, dying in the heat of the noonday sun.

"How sad," he thought, "that thousands have to die. It's too bad there are so many. One man cannot save them all."

The man continued his walk down the beach, and soon he passed a very old bare-footed woman who was picking up starfish, one by one, and throwing them back into the sea.

"My dear woman," said the strolling man. "Why are you throwing those starfish back into the sea? Can't you see there are many thousands? You can't even make a dent in the number of starfish that will die today. What difference are your efforts going to make?"

The old woman picked up another starfish and threw it into the sea, then replied, "It's going to make a difference to this one."

"That's a beautiful story," Mary said, "but why are you telling it to me?"

"Because I am the starfish; you are the woman who threw me into the sea, and I want to thank you for doing it."

"Oh yes," I added. "There is one more thing."

"What?" she asked.

I reached down and moved my queen.

"Checkmate," I smiled.

The most powerful principle I ever discovered was compound interest.
--Albert Einstein

Interest

Mary probably thought she wouldn't see me anymore, now that I didn't need her money. But she was wrong. She had opened a whole new world of opportunity for me, and I was determined to learn all I could from her. We continued to play chess, usually two or three times a month. Usually she won, but I won, too, because I always came away with some new idea or understanding that would help me along my way to financial prosperity. Interest became one of our favorite topics of discussion.

Interest is a formidable opponent. Once the game starts, he never rests. You may work 50 or 60 hours a week to keep up with him, but he works 168 hours a week to keep ahead of you. He never takes a timeout or a half-time break.

He works every Sunday, every holiday, and every night. He has no mercy. He even takes your money when you are sick in bed. And if you lose your job and miss two payments, he will take your house.

Chequemate

If you have a $100,000 mortgage on your home at 8%, you can go to sleep every night knowing you just accrued another $22 in interest. You pay $22 when you spend Christmas day at Grandma's. You pay another $22 every Sunday, even when you are in church. When you signed the papers for that $100,000 30-year mortgage, you agreed to pay $164,153 in interest. Add closing costs and occasional late fees, and you will almost pay for your house three times by the time the mortgage is paid.

Everyone needs to know how much interest he or she is paying, and be aware of the options available to drastically cut interest payments. For example, if you increased the payment on the above $100,000 mortgage by $222 a month, which would enable you to pay it off in 15 instead of 30 years, your total interest expense would be $72,017 instead of $164,153, a savings of $92,136. That's a lot of money, enough to supplement your Social Security check very nicely after you retire.

If you finance a new car over five years at 12% interest, you just about pay for it twice. And what about the 18 % you pay on VISA and MasterCard, unpaid medical and dental bills, and so on? If you had a $3900 balance on your VISA or MasterCard, and you paid the minimum payment of $78 a month, it would take 35 years to pay the balance down to zero, assuming you never used the card again. During that time you would have paid $10,096 in interest.

If you add up all the interest you are paying, including your mortgage, you can begin to see why you are struggling financially, even with a good job or a double income. Just think what you could do if you got to keep all that money you spend in interest every month. In my case, eliminating my interest payments was like getting a $1,000 a month tax-free raise.

I'm not suggesting that the bankers be hauled off to jail. If your banker helps you get into a fourplex apartment where your rental income is $1,800 a month, and your payment to the bank is $1,200 a month, and you'll own the thing free and clear in 12 years, that's a good deal, and you ought to give your banker a hug.

The general guideline for borrowing, endorsed by most financial planners, is that you borrow for things that increase in value or produce income, never for things that depreciate. *Borrow for business, and to buy assets that increase in value, but pay cash for pleasure, comfort and vanity.*

For those who spend their way out of debt, interest can suddenly become a wonderful teammate. Instead of being a borrower, you are a lender. Instead of being in the interest trap, interest is working just as hard for you as it used to work against you. Twenty four hours a day, seven days a week, it is earning money for you. It works weekends, holidays, and nights. It never takes a day off, and it earns just as much for you on the days when you are sick as when you are well, and just as much when you are on vacation as when you are working. *Those who don't understand interest, pay it. Those who understand it, collect it.* After Albert Einstein invented the atomic bomb, he said the most powerful thing he ever discovered was compound interest.

A person or couple earning a lifetime income of $2 million (about $45,000 a year), taking 30-year mortgage and always paying minimum payments on bills will pay $300,000 to $400,000 in interest.

Over a 45 year working career, $200,000 in interest breaks down to about $370 a month.

Suppose you invested $370 a month at 6% instead of paying it out, the amount you'd end up with is $1,045,232 in the bank when you retire. By continuing to earn 6%, you could withdraw $5336 a month during retirement, and never reduce the principal.

Now try this scenario. If you could come up with just another $30 a month and invest $400 a month for your entire working life, and earn an average of 9% interest on it, your nest egg would add up to $2,984,166 by the time you retire and you could draw out $22,381 a month for the rest of your life, without reducing principal.

As you make modest increases in your savings, the impact over your lifetime will be dramatic. The point is that *if you can just change the direction of your interest stream so it's coming in instead of going out, you will see wonderful, far-reaching changes in your financial life.*

Mary was helping me get out of the interest trap, helping me make the transition from borrower to lender. And I was doing it without earning more money, and certainly without robbing a bank or winning the lottery.

One reason most of us are borrowers instead of lenders is that we are too easily seduced by easy credit plans which make it possible to have the things we want now, and not have to pay for them until later. Once we get on the interest/installment treadmill, it seems impossible to get off. Sure, we can get the things we want without having to pay up front, but is it worth it when we feel poor all the time?

Most of us can't afford to pay for our home three times, but we hardly hesitate signing documents to make sure we do just that. When we enter a store to buy something with an 18% APR credit card, if the clerk, upon seeing the card, automatically increased the price of the item by 50%, we probably wouldn't buy the item. But, that is exactly the price we are paying, if we add the interest we will pay before the amount charged to the card has been paid off.

Too many Americans are already spending more than they earn each month, using three or four credit cards, or home equity lines of credit, to make up the difference. It isn't unusual for the outstanding balance on those cards to be over $10,000 requiring $150 a month in interest payments alone.

When we graduated from high school, most of us, including me, had dreams of making as much as we do now, but thought we would be affluent and happy on that much income, not trapped in a frantic struggle from one paycheck to the next.

Interest

We wonder why we had fewer money problems when we were earning a third of what we earn now. Worrying over money is more likely to cause high blood pressure than salt. Money worries sap vitality and break up families. Nothing robs us of our self esteem quicker than bills we can't pay.

If the people in Bangladesh knew how much you and I were earning, they would call us Rockefellers. A college professor with a Ph.D. in Mongolia earns the equivalent of about $200 a month. Per capita income is only $350 USD per year in China, and they manage to save a higher percentage of their income than Americans do. We should count our blessings. Instead we are frantically paddling a leaky canoe across an ocean of red ink, fearful that if we stop, the canoe will sink.

You may earn $2.5 million in your lifetime, but when you retire, if you're average, you will have $8,700 in savings, enough to last about six months when you are expected to live another 17 years.

Some find solace, thinking the federal government will take care of us. After all, we have Social Security and Medicare.

The problem is our federal government doesn't have any more fiscal discipline than most of its debt-crazy citizens. Our government is the biggest debtor of all.

The truth is that this country has been involved in an outrageous international buying spree. We buy foreign cars, clothes, electronics, and thousands of other products resulting in a monster money imbalance with our trade partners. An incredible amount of our wealth and productivity has been transferred to Japan. We have exported whole industrial segments including textiles, semiconductors, ship building, electronic fabrication, industrial machinery production, even steel making.

Following the lead set by George Washington when he threw a silver dollar over the Potomac River, our modern presidents have thrown many billions of dollars over the Pacific and Atlantic Oceans -- money that will never come back.

At the same time, the national debt has soared. For the first time in the nation's history we depend on individual and institutional investors from Japan and Germany to buy our government bonds to finance our national debt. A third of our income is used to make interest payments to those investors. In one short decade, we have gone from the world's largest lending nation to the world's biggest borrower.

When the '91 recession hit, driving unemployment to 7.9%, foreclosures soared, real estate prices on both coasts fell, the divorce rate increased, and the families that had savings were forced to spend them. Many watched the value of their homes drop below the outstanding balances on their mortgages.

How did Americans respond to the recession? Did they become more frugal, more conservative, more determined to get out of debt and save money?

We did the opposite of what was required. In 1993, the savings rate dropped to an all-time low in this country, to 0.6% of Gross Domestic Product, the lowest since World War II. In the meantime, the Germans were saving 14% of their domestic production, the Japanese 20%, and the British 15%.

We passed N.A.F.T.A. (North American Free Trade Agreement), allowing a whole new wave of foreign products to flood our markets, and a new river of U.S. dollars to leave the country. As Canadian beef stampeded in, the price of feeder cattle in the U.S. dropped to half of what it was before N.A.F.T.A., crippling a large segment of our livestock industry.

And how did the American people respond to the recession? Instead of taking a hard look at how they managed their money, the only response was to vote the Republicans out of the White House, and the Democrats out of Congress. Otherwise it was business as usual, with the national debt taking another big jump.

Fifty-five percent of the citizens of the richest country in the history of the world have a zero or negative net worth.

Interest

In 1995 the federal government ran out of money twice, and was forced to shut down, except for essential services. Would you buy stock in a company that had to cease its operations for lack of money twice in a single year? Would you trust 100% of the responsibility for your retirement income in the hands of a company that had to shut down twice in one year? Yet, that is exactly what most of us are doing by leaving the responsibility for retirement income and medical care in the hands of the government.

Mary said that as long as the federal government stays in business, there will probably be some kind of Social Security and Medicare payments, but how good can these services be when the number of retired people over 65 doubles, as it will by the year 2030? Government and private pensions will be severely tested when they have to sustain 76 million aging baby boomers, many of whom will spend as many years in retirement as they did working.

Today there are 3.4 workers for every Social Security beneficiary. By 2035 the ratio will be 1.9 to 1. In other words, workers will have to be taxed twice as much as they are today just to maintain the present level of benefits to future Social Security recipients. Do you think taxpayers and voters will happily support a 100% increase in the FICA tax? They never have in the past, and they certainly won't in the future. We have never been here before, so no one knows exactly what is going to happen. Conditions are different than before the Great Depression. On the one hand, our present-day economists seem more sophisticated and more adept at manipulating the economy to avoid disaster. On the other hand, people without money can't turn to the land for sustenance the way their parents and grandparents did in the Great Depression. It is entirely possible that a modern collapse would be a lot worse than the one in the thirties.

So when are Americans going to learn that, even though

they can have just about *anything* they need, they can't have *everything* they want? When are baby boomers going to learn that denial is not a river in Egypt? When will they start treating their money as a precious resource, as they do the owls, whales, and rain forests?

An investment counselor was surprised when an aging couple, 97 and 98 years old, entered his office to see about starting payments into a retirement fund. "Why did you wait so long?" the counselor asked.

"Couldn't afford it while the children were alive," they responded.

The real tragedy is that many of the people in the interest-debt trap didn't get there through ignorance and stupidity. Most of the baby boomers grew up in homes where they were taught, or at least observed sound financial practices -- paying off mortgages in years instead of decades, saving for rainy days, establishing savings accounts for college, putting money away for retirement.

If people know something about handling money, why don't they do it better? And if they don't know anything, why don't painful interest payments motivate them to take the courses, buy the books, and listen to the tapes on getting out of debt and achieving financial prosperity?

Everybody *wants* to be out of debt. Everybody would rather collect interest than pay interest. Try to find someone who says he or she is perfectly content to retire on nothing more than Social Security. There are no such people. Then, why are most of us headed for a place where none of us want to be?

If the know-how is available on how to achieve financial security, why don't people do it? Why do we find it so hard to resist all the convincing advertising aimed at getting us to buy things we cannot afford and don't really need? Why are we tempted by those offers for easy credit again and again? Why would we rather drive luxury sports cars now, than have $300,000 worth of mutual funds when we retire? Are we really

Interest

that short-sighted, that stupid?

Have you ever watched hungry children dig into big pieces of German chocolate cake? One child will eat the cake first and save the frosting until last. Another child will eat the frosting first, then the cake. Some like to save the best until last. Others eat the best part first. Adults are the same way. If you bring home a video to watch after dinner, do you clean up the dinner dishes before you watch the video, or after?

We're talking about delayed gratification, scheduling pain before pleasure, work before play, toil before rest. It's the way our parents and grandparents lived during the depression because bitter experience taught them it was the only way to survive. They had the old-fashioned belief that money should be earned before it could be spent. They were in a generation where one ate the cake before the frosting. We live in a generation where too many people eat the frosting first.

We believe the salesman when he says you might as well put the item on the charge account so you can enjoy it while you are paying for it. What he doesn't say is that by buying on credit, if you add the interest to the cost of the item, you will be paying a much higher price for the object.

The businessman who puts the hard tasks at the top of his "to do" list and attacks them first accomplishes much more in a day than the person who saves the difficult tasks until last. Usually he or she never gets to the more difficult tasks, and, unfortunately, these are usually the most important items on any list. *Delaying gratification is the process of scheduling the pain and pleasure in life in such a way as to make the pleasure better by facing the pain first and getting it over with.*

People would rather go to movies, play basketball, go out to dinner, or just putter in the garden than work on finances -- pay bills, balance registers, discuss budgeting and expenditure decisions. Such tasks are generally perceived as unpleasant, even painful, and because attention to personal finances is not

93

required by law, except at tax time, such matters are either postponed, or neglected altogether.

But, if you stop and think about it, the discomfort associated in wrestling with financial problems now is nothing compared to the pain, hurt and downright misery associated with foreclosure, bankruptcy, and facing years of retirement with nothing more than Social Security. By avoiding a little effort, now we are inviting a lot of pain later on.

It's like the child who is having so much fun playing that he tries to ignore the growing discomfort in his bladder. He knows it's time to interrupt his play and go to the bathroom, but he's having too much fun. He continues to postpone the trip to the bathroom until what would have been only a minor interruption turns into a major inconvenience, requiring him to stop play altogether because he has to go home to bathe and find clean clothes.

This book presents better and more efficient ways to handle money. Too many people associate money management with unpleasant words like deprivation, denial, cutting back, belt- tightening, budgeting. It is just as easy to associate money management with pleasant words like spending, buying, shopping, dividends, peace of mind, and accomplishment. It is time we change the way we look at money. Buying mutual funds can be almost as much fun as buying a sports car.

Just about everybody reaches the point in life where he or she realizes his income is about as high as it is ever going to get, and he is still a long way from feeling financially secure.

The truth is, you don't have to make a lot of money to become financially secure. All you need is a program that enables you to redirect the way you spend the income already in place, in a way that gets you out of debt, and helps you accumulate sufficient assets to take care of you until the day you die. If this is what you want, following the principles presented in these pages will get you there.

Financial security is more a function of how you spend, than how much money you earn.
--Blaine Harris

Spending

I reviewed my targets on a daily basis, and when each paycheck arrived, I paid myself first by taking 10% off the top to pay down the debt with the lowest remaining balance.

Once we were used to living on 90%t of my income, we didn't even miss the other 10%. It didn't seem like very long at all until the home equity loan was paid off, and the only remaining debt was the mortgage, and making triple payments on the house made me feel like General Norman Schwartzkopf leading the charge in the Gulf War.

About this time, I surprised Mary by announcing that I wanted to write a book that would contain all the things she was teaching me. I was sincere when I told her that other people deserved the opportunity to know and understand the four laws, too, and I thought the best way to share would be in the pages of a book.

"What makes you think a furniture salesman can write a

book?" she asked. Her question didn't catch me by surprise. I
had been asking myself the same thing for about a month.

"You should see the love letters I used to write to Judy,"
I teased. We both laughed. Then I got serious. "It's not like I'm
trying to write circles around Michael Crichton, or scare Steven
King to death," I said. "All I want to do is write down the things
I learned from you, so others can learn, too. I had to do a little bit
of writing to graduate from college. I got A's in some of my
English classes, and I'm an avid reader. I believe I can do it.
Tom Clancy sold insurance before he hit the best-seller lists.
John Grisham was a lawyer."

"Someday they'll be saying Paul Smith was a furniture
salesman," she added. "What will you call the book?"

"*Spending Your Way to Wealth,*" I said, expressing the
idea that creating wealth is not so much a function of budgeting
and belt-tightening as it is the result of spending differently,
spending your money to get out of debt and investing in assets
that appreciate.

"I don't know if I like it," Mary said. "First of all, it
sounds too much like *Sinning Your Way to Heaven,* or *Eating
Your Way to Thinness.*"

I reminded her that there are diets in which people lose
weight, not by eating less, but by eating differently. They make
changes in the kinds of foods they eat -- less gravy, French fries,
ice cream, and prime rib; more broccoli, grapefruit, cottage
cheese, sprouts and fish.

Spending, like eating, involves an infinite number of
choices. While schools teach our children basic nutritional
principles involved in eating, they do not do a very good job of
teaching our children the basic spending principles needed for
financial survival in a world of money.

"Almost anyone with steady employment, regardless of
income level, upon learning correct spending principles, can
spend his or her way out of debt and achieve financial prosperity
in about five years," she said. "When you buy something of

value, you receive an instruction manual telling you how to care for that product to insure maximum use and longevity. But, have you ever heard of an employer giving out instruction booklets with pay checks?"

I told Mary this book would be an instruction book for pay checks, a guidebook for spending. The readers who followed the principles outlined in the pages of our book would be able to achieve debt-free prosperity in about five years, or less. They would also learn how to build substantial nest eggs for retirement, if that's what they wanted to do.

"Maybe we can show a few people that the financial dreams they didn't think were possible," she added, "are really within their grasp."

"After reading the book they will have the tools to achieve those dreams," I added.

"In my years at the IRS, I saw some good money management, but more bad money management," Mary said. "A small number of families always seemed to have money available for college educations, down payments for children's homes, small businesses, and retirement. While most families with similar incomes always seemed to be struggling just to pay their bills, and never seemed to be more than 60 days away from bankruptcy."

"A book like this needs to be written," she added. "A handbook for pay checks that would show everyone, including our children, in a very logical and convincing way, how to get organized financially, how to get the most out of the money they earn, how to get out of debt and become financially secure on any income."

The mission of this book is to help people achieve worthy financial goals by presenting well-conceived, easy-to-use methods for *tracking* expenses, setting *targets*, *trimming* expenses, and *training* readers in the art of spending money wisely. In this book we reveal and teach the time-tested secrets used by normal people, at every income level, to achieve debt-free prosperity.

Financial security is more a function of how you spend, than how much money you earn.

Too many people have the false belief that the single biggest cause of financial stress is earning too little money. "If I only earned another $400 a month, I wouldn't have these problems."

What would happen if the president of the United States, during a re-election campaign, appeared on television one night to announce that in order to relieve the financial pressure on individuals and families, he was ordering all companies, effective immediately, to give their employees a 10% across-the-board wage and salary increase?

What would be the consequence of such an action? The president would get re-elected, for sure, but in six months would there be less financial stress in America? No. Instead of using the extra 10% to pay off debts, or increase savings, most people would take the extra money and make a down payment on a new Dodge truck, or the boat they always wanted, and increase their debt burden even more. *The lack of money doesn't cause as much financial stress as the lack of ability to spend our money wisely.*

Mary told me that years ago she had a friend in Montana. His name was Mike, and he was building an attractive log home on one of the most beautiful hilltops in the scenic Bitterroot Valley. Mike was debt-free, and his only income was the hourly wage he earned at the Forest Service.

"When I got out of school, I landed a good job and spent every penny," Mike explained. "But I wasn't happy, so I dropped out and became a hippie. I earned nothing and lived on nothing. I wasn't happy living that way, either. So I got another job, but continued living on nothing like during my hippie days. I was driving a $150 car, and my wife bought clothes at Goodwill.

"It wasn't long until I was able to buy ten acres of good land," he continued. "Then I started building the house, paying cash for the building materials. When it is finished, it will be mine. If I lose my job, I won't lose my house and land. In fact, if I lose my job, my land will provide for my family."

He had an orchard, a large garden, chickens and a cow. Mike worked hard, but enjoyed financial peace of mind.

We know a lot of people who say they would like to trade places with Mike. What they don't seem to understand is what Mike has is within the grasp of almost anyone with a steady job, as long as they understand they can have *anything* they need, but not *everything* they want. "Any fool can get money, but it takes a wise man to keep it," Mary added.

She told me about Julio's friends who worked on the big cattle and sheep ranches. Most of them speak very little English. Most are from Mexico or Peru. She said Americans generally don't want these herding jobs because the pay is only $700 a month, and the hours are long. Cows and sheep need to be looked after on weekends and holidays, during the night, too.

"Why do the workers from Mexico and Peru want these jobs?" Mary asked. "You assume the answer lies in the horrid financial conditions in their home countries. Not necessarily so. Just like Julio, each herder receives room and board in addition to his $700 a month. He has few opportunities to go into town and spend money. A single man without large family obligations at home can do like Julio, and save $500 a month. After five years, he can buy a printing press, take it home and have a means to support a family for the rest of his life. Or, he can buy a nice piece of land to sustain his children and grand children long after he is gone. No wonder those workers from Peru and Mexico are lined up at the emigration office. They see those $700-a-month herding jobs as opportunities to save $500 a month."

If a herder earning $700 a month can save enough to become a comparatively wealthy landowner or businessman, when he returns to his own country, maybe the rest us who are earning three, four, five or ten times that much ought to quit believing the only solution to our financial woes is to make more money.

Ask Mary's friend, Mike, if it's possible to own a beautiful debt-free home on a scenic piece of land earning only $8 an hour at the Forest Service. *If Mike and the Peruvians on their tiny incomes can get ahead financially, the rest of us ought to be able to do it, too.* But it takes management, discipline, the kind you have been reading about in this book. It's not as hard as you think. Help is available. The principles are simple.

*1. **Track** your daily expenses by writing them down.*
*2. **Target** realistic financial goals, write them down, and imprint them in your internal computer.*
*3. **Trim** your living expenses so you live on less than you earn, then spend the difference to get out of debt and buy assets that appreciate. Pay yourself first.*
*4. **Train.** Discover the power of compound interest. Learn investment strategies for stocks, securities, real estate. Develop a long-term relationship with a financial advisor.*

Mary told me about a Vietnamese couple who arrived penniless in San Francisco in the mid-1980s. They obtained minimum-wage work in a donut shop. Being without any financial resources, they were allowed to stay in a back room. Leftover food was provided to them.

After several years they had the opportunity to get an apartment. The American dream was finally within reach. But, thinking it over, realizing that with the apartment they would have to pay utilities, buy a car, appliances, furniture, insurance, and groceries, they decided to stay in the back room and live on leftovers for two more years.

When they had been in the country five years, they bought the restaurant where they had been working. They paid $30,000, cash. They had saved 80% of the money they had earned. Today they own many restaurants.

Too many Americans spend 104% of their income, using

easy credit to go a little deeper in debt each month. The average American has less than $1,000 in savings, and is less than 90 days from foreclosure and bankruptcy if his or her income were to stop. Worrying about money is a leading cause of stress-related heart failure. And fighting about money is the leading cause of divorce.

Everybody seems so concerned about our precious natural resources -- air, water, fossil fuels, rain forests, even whales and owls. But, what about our money? Isn't it about time we started treating it as a precious resource? If you don't, you'll wish you had if you ever get a pink slip and have no reserve to fall back on, or when you get that gold watch and realize you'll be facing the golden years in poverty while your friends are spending their winters in Arizona and Florida.

Working harder and longer is not the answer. A new idea, a new way of doing business is needed. That's what this book is about.

It doesn't matter if you are earning $15,000 a year and feel like you are paddling a leaky canoe, or earning $150,000 a year and driving a sinking house boat. The feeling is the same if you can't pay your bills and realize your ocean of debt is getting deeper and deeper. If you feel like you need a financial miracle, and don't think you are going to win the lottery any time soon, this book can show you what to do.

Most people have a very simple system for managing their money. They put their pay check in the bank, pay the required bills, and hope the rest lasts until the next pay check. Of course, it doesn't. And when asked where the money went, they respond in broad, sweeping generalities because they have no clear picture of what happened to the money.

People seem to want to blame everyone else for their financial woes. "My employer is too cheap to pay a decent wage." "Shoddy government management is ruining Social Security." "Greedy landlords charge too much rent." "The IRS is stealing my money." "If American manufacturers were more concerned with quality than profit, I wouldn't have to spend so much money replacing all the stuff that breaks -- I wouldn't be throwing away more dollars than people in India live on."

Who can you blame when you turn 65 and don't have enough saved up to get through a single year of retirement?

Who can you blame if the daughter you love so much wants to get a college education and you can't afford to help her?

If you don't know who to blame for your financial woes, look in a mirror.

It doesn't have to be this way. Responsible spending, regardless of your income level, can enable you to get the things you need and want.

The simple truth is that in the absence of a spending plan with clearly defined goals and a method of tracking money, Americans will spend whatever they earn, sometimes more, thanks to easy credit. The person earning $25,000 a year spends it all. The person earning $50,000 a year spends it all. The person earning $75,000 a year spends it all.

The first step in getting control of your spending is to start **tracking**, keeping a record of every dollar you spend on a daily basis and writing it down.

The next step is to set realistic **targets.** You can't create a plan to go somewhere if you don't know where you want to go.

Next, you have to **trim** your spending habits so that you live on less than you earn. You don't have to do like the Vietnamese couple and live on 20% of earnings, but if you can live on 90%, if you are typical, wonderful things can happen in your life.

If the $25,000 per year wage earner forces himself to live on $22,500, he will hardly notice the difference. Likewise, the $50,000 wage earner won't have to give up much to live on $45,000, or the $75,000 person to live on $67,500. But they will all notice amazing changes in their financial problems. Their money worries will disappear because they have money in the bank, and the knowledge that they are progressing towards desirable financial goals -- getting out of debt, building a retirement annuity, saving for their daughter's college, etc.

And because they don't want to suffer setbacks through bad investments, they are constantly reading, asking questions, and learning. This we call **training.**

It is entirely possible for almost anyone on any income to live debt-free, and to collect interest instead of pay it.

In the recent version of the movie, *Sabrina,* starring Harrison Ford, the aging chauffeur, Fairchild, surprises his daughter with the announcement that, over the years, by staying home and reading books, and making careful investments, he has accumulated over $2 million for her.

"Only in the movies," you might say. Not so. News reports on people like Fairchild are almost commonplace, like the one about a retiring postal worker who had accumulated $4.2 million in real estate investments. Just before this book went to press, there was a piece on television about a cleaning lady who donated over half a million dollars to start a scholarship fund for needy black women.

When Anne Schreiber died at age 101 in 1995, *Money Magazine* ran an article describing how this retired IRS worker had turned $5,000 in savings into a $22,000,000 fortune which she left to charity.

Eating is something we have to do every day. If we do it wrong, we can weigh in at 220 pounds. If we do it right, we can weigh in at 175 or 125 pounds. As long as we are going to eat, we might as well do it right. As long as we are going to spend, we might as well do that right, too.

Spending is like eating. We have to do it every day. We can't stop spending any more than we can stop eating. If we spend right, we can live debt-free with surplus money going into investment vehicles which pay for our children's educations and allow us to retire in comfort. It's the only decent way to live. On the other hand, if we spend irresponsibly, we always seem to be a dollar short, worrying about money, and have too little to retire on when we can no longer work.

As long as we are going to spend, we might as well do it right. *This book shows how anyone on any income can spend their way to debt-free prosperity.* Like Mary must have said to me a hundred times, "Now it's your move."

Learning the disciplines necessary to manage small amounts of money is the secret to the accumulation and management of large amounts of money.
--Blaine Harris

Chequemate®

I'll never forget my last conversation with Mary. She was having serious heart problems which were making it increasingly difficult for her to live by herself. She had decided to move to Oklahoma City to live with her daughter.

"This is your last chance if you want any of that $2 million dollars," she said in a teasing voice. But, I knew she wasn't teasing. If I wanted to borrow all or part of that money, I had no doubts about her willingness to give it to me.

"I'm going to miss you," I said.

"You'll do just fine. You've learned your lessons well. Now that you can't spend so much time playing chess with me, maybe you'll finish the book."

"I have a serious concern about the book," I said, moving over to the sofa and arranging the pawns on the board.

"Tell me about it."

"A book can't replace Mary Sessions," I said.

Chequemate

"What is that supposed to mean?"

"I could never have gotten control of my financial life without your help."

"I know," she said, confidently.

"The regular meetings, going over the work sheets, making commitments, reporting back -- a book can't do those kinds of things. For the readers to benefit as I have, they need a Mary Sessions."

"You're not suggesting that I let you put my name and phone number in the back of your book so ten thousand people will call me, asking for a $2 million line of credit?" she asked.

"No. I'm just afraid that if the readers don't have a Mary Sessions, they won't be able to do what I did."

"The principles are the same, whether they read them in a book or hear them while playing chess with me," she argued.

I had to agree. "But," I insisted, " once the principles are mastered, the key to applying them is consistency." How many times have you been excited about a new diet, or exercise program, or learning a new sport or skill? You make a commitment to do it every day -- only to be distracted a few weeks down the road. You remember a month later that you are no longer doing what you decided to do.

If you get into a debt elimination program to be free of debt in three years, and you set aside an extra $200 a month for accelerated debt payments, if you forget to do it in the fourth and fifth months, how successful will you be in getting out of debt?

You never see this lack of consistency in college and professional sports. You never hear about a player forgetting to go to practice a few weeks into the season. There are coaches to make sure that doesn't happen. You never read about a tight end who forgot what time he was supposed to be playing in the Super Bowl, or the point guard who was so involved in watching videos, he missed the tipoff of the game with the San Antonio Spurs.

In team sports, the game dates are scheduled years in

Chequemate

advance. The players, coaches, media and many of the fans schedule their lives around dates etched in steel. You never hear about a football team deciding to play Monday night football on Tuesday because nobody wanted to miss the re-broadcast of *Roots*.

Mary agreed that the consistency we see in sports is the same kind required to be successful in any financial management plan. She said the power of compound interest reaches atomic proportions when a player is consistent, not just month after month, and year after year, but decade upon decade.

Calvin Coolidge said, *"Nothing in the world can take the place of persistence. Talent will not; nothing is more common than unsuccessful men with talent. Genius will not; unrewarded genius is almost a proverb. Education will not; the world is full of educated derelicts. Persistence and determination alone are omnipotent. The slogan 'press on' has solved, and always will solve the problems of the human race."*

A 15-year-old can earn a million dollars by retirement by saving seven dollars a month. A 17-year old can earn $2.4 million by retirement by putting away a dollar a day at 12%. Our teenagers spend $99 billion a year, and $63 billion of it is their own money. Millions of them can afford to save a dollar a day, and all of them could save $7 a month to be millionaires at retirement.

If every teenager was required to read this book, some would start savings programs. But for every hundred who did, after six months, only two or three would still be doing it. It is human nature to be lazy and forgetful. Most of us need help if we are to be determined and persistent over a long period of time.

Athletes aren't any better than the rest of us. They don't miss their games because schedules are imposed upon them, and they have coaches to prod them.

Mary said the best way to insure consistency in a financial plan is to widen the circle of commitment. Consistency at anything over long periods of time is tough if you are alone or in a vacuum. Corporations and millionaires overcome this by hiring teams of accountants and auditing firms to keep track of their dollars.

"Private individuals can do that, too," Mary said. "And, at a very reasonable price."

"I never heard of anything like that," I said.

"I've told you about it before," she insisted.

"No you haven't. I would have remembered."

"Almost every time we've played chess, I said the name," she teased.

I was really confused. I had no idea what she was talking about.

"Checkmate," she said.

I had to agree. She had said that many times, too many times.

"The name of the company is Chequemate International®," she said. "It offers a complete package of financial management services to individuals, families and home businesses, complete with monthly reports, counseling sessions, investment seminars, and a newsletter."

"Is it expensive?"

"Less than the cost of a night out for dinner once a month. Anyone can afford that in exchange for financial stability."

I had to laugh, thinking how strange it was that Mary always seemed to find a way to end our conversations, even this last and final one, with the word *Chequemate*. Maybe that would be a good name for the new book.

Chequemate -- The next move is yours...

The Chequemate Challenge

Chequemate challenges each of us to make a difference. We are each on the chessboard of life. We must assume the responsibility for ourselves and those who depend on us and make them our number one business interest. We must then manage that activity with business intensity which must drive every move we make in order to achieve self-reliance and complete financial independence.

Chequemate has created tracking tools and monthly reporting services for individuals, as well as small businesses to help them succeed at whatever level they choose.

Chequemate has also developed a savings program designed to generate additional savings necessary to fund family priorities. This savings program allows individuals to share with others the secrets of money they have learned through the Chequemate system.

Call 1-800-CHK-MATE (1-800-245-6283) for more information on additional services or visit us on the internet at www.chkmate.com.

Chequemate

After reading this book, it is pretty hard to continue with excuses about your financial future. There is almost no excuse for anyone being out of control with their finances. It should be a high school class and required reading for all high school students.
--Pat & Vicki Dillon, Pavi Enterprises,
Mission Viejo, California

This is a tremendous resource. I will not hesitate to present it to newlyweds, millionaires and all those in between.
--Ray Quinn, Ph.D, CLU, CFP, St. Paul, Minnesota

Had I been introduced to your book in my youth, I would have been motivated to an informed "Proactive Want to Spend More Wisely Attitude" and would be enjoying a luxurious retirement right now.
--Virgil Beasley, Psychologist, Healdsburg, California

I found this book to be both inspirational and financially beneficial. A "real" gem.
--Lauri Weiss-Rimler, Advertising Sales Executive,
New Providence, New Jersey

In today's society, money has become the primary source of marital dissention and divorce. The principles taught in *The Four Laws of Debt Free Prosperity,* when practiced, will eliminate money as the chief cause of divorce. This book should be given as a wedding gift to every newlywed couple.
--Carolyn Fife, Travel Writer, Murray, Utah

Thanks for the book. You bring a great message to those who desire to be in the group of the "haves" versus "have nots". Good luck and God bless.
--Jon Stiglaino, Marketing Director, Leadership
Management, Inc., Waco, Texas

110

Chequemate

The message in *The Four Laws* is so simple yet so powerful. This easy to follow guide about getting out of debt and staying out of debt makes it exciting to think about the possibilities of accumulating wealth by eliminating debt.
--Hal Glick, VP, Moore, Warfield & Glick Realtors, Inc., Ocean City, Maryland

I'm 52. If your book had been required reading in school, I would have achieved financial security years ago and our country wouldn't be collapsing under debt.
--Richard Quinn, Attorney, Honolulu, Hawaii

Had the system described in this book been available 30 years ago, I could have earned half the money and created twice as much wealth. This is the best book for family finances I have ever encountered.
--Michael Vavrinec, CEO Select Enterprises, Sisters, Oregon

After one month of use, Chequemate is paid for through the end of the year because of tax deductions -- pretty incredible!
--Wendy Christensen, public relations, Mandala Agency, Bend, Oregon

I have spent sixteen years helping small businesses simplify their bookkeeping procedures. Chequemate is the "Kitty Hawk" of cash management systems. It takes cash management to a higher level.
--Bruce Cameron, Safeguard Distributor, Orem, Utah

The System described in this book has changed my spending habits. I now keep more money in my pocket and spend less time keeping track of my money; I don't have to make a double entry with each transaction like I did with Quicken.
--Forrest Silver, Exec. Manager, Ellicott City, Maryland

111

Notes

Comments   Page No.

Notes

Comments   Page No.